THE STORY OF MORE

HOW WE GOT TO CLIMATE CHANGE
AND WHERE TO GO FROM HERE

ADAPTED FOR YOUNG ADULTS

HOPE JAHREN

DELACORTE PRESS

FOR MY MOTHER
AND
BECAUSE OF MY FATHER

All rights reserved. Published in the United States by Delacorte Press,
an imprint of Random House Children's Books, a division
of Penguin Random House LLC, New York.

This work is based on *The Story of More: How We Got to Climate Change and Where
to Go from Here*, published in paperback by Vintage Books, a division of Penguin
Random House LLC, New York, in 2020.

Delacorte Press is a registered trademark and the colophon
is a trademark of Penguin Random House LLC.

Visit us on the Web! GetUnderlined.com

Educators and librarians, for a variety of teaching tools,
visit us at RHTeachersLibrarians.com

Library of Congress Cataloging-in-Publication Data is available upon request.
ISBN 978-0-593-38112-0 (trade) — ISBN 978-0-593-38113-7 (lib. bdg.) —
ISBN 978-0-593-38114-4 (ebook)

The text of this book is set in 11.5-point Alkes.
Interior design by Ken Crossland

Printed in the United States of America
10 9 8 7 6 5 4 3 2 1
First Edition

CONTENTS

A NOTE FROM THE AUTHOR

The first edition of this book was released on March 3, 2020 and was released for an adult audience.

During the same week that *The Story of More* was released, the number of people testing positive for COVID-19 worldwide first exceeded one thousand per day. Just two weeks later, that number increased to ten thousand per day. Before the end of the month, the United States had reported over one hundred thousand cases of COVID-19 within its borders alone, and all of Europe was effectively locked down. In Norway, the country where I live, our workplaces were shut, our children's schools were closed, and use of public transportation was limited to medical and other civil workers. We spent our days at home, leaving only to visit the grocery store or pharmacy. I was terrified for myself and for my family, but I was also hopeful that the take-home recommendation of my book *Use Less, Share More* could play a key role in getting through the pandemic.

Throughout 2020, global societies shifted between the status of locked-down and openly functioning, with many spending months going back and forth and living in-between. International air travel was effectively halted for much of 2020, and both working and learning at home became common. Our everyday activities gave us the impression that the transportation of people and the manufacture and shipping of goods by car, truck, plane, or boat decreased radically during 2020. Because industry and transport produced the lion's share of greenhouse gases prior to COVID-19, many scientists were eager to learn whether the total amount of these gases in the atmosphere (particularly carbon dioxide, that is CO_2) was lower in 2020 compared to 2019.

Unfortunately, it was not. The average amount of CO_2 in the atmosphere during 2020 was 414 parts per million ("ppm" is the unit used for measurement), while the average for 2019 was lower: 412 ppm. Not only that, but in 2018 the value was 409 ppm, in 2017 it was 407 ppm, in 2016 it was 404 ppm, and in 2015 it was 401 ppm. This means that for the last five years, the amount of CO_2 has increased steadily by 2 to 3 ppm each year, and 2020 was no exception. We know that the cycling of gases in and out of the atmosphere is complex, but two things have become clear—first, that the massive disruption to our lives brought on by COVID-19 during 2020 did not translate into a massive decrease of CO_2 in our atmosphere. Second, that any effects were likely more subtle and will be expressed on longer time-scales than we can appreciate at this moment. There's another possibility, too: maybe all of our life changes in 2020 added up to no more than an imperceptible baby step toward a reduction in global energy use, indicating that real environmental progress will require much greater sacrifices. I can promise you this: scientists will be studying the effect of the 2020 shutdown on our environment for a very long time.

None of this changes the fact that, for very many of us, our daily energy use decreased during 2020. I am often asked whether we will go back to consuming as much energy, waste as much food, or harm the environment as much as we used to, after society someday returns to "normal" post-COVID-19. I can't predict the future (and you shouldn't trust people who think they can), but I do know this: that the *majority* of the driving and meeting and buying and flying and shopping and traveling before 2020—the things we had done for years because they were necessary, for our jobs, for our families, for our lives—so many of them turned out to be *optional*. For better or worse, or for even better or even worse, we've gone months without constantly appealing to the habits that the last fifty years of consumption drilled into us, and we mostly survived. This can be a firm foundation for truly transformative change, if we can be brave enough to believe such change is possible.

At present, the COVID-19 epidemic is no longer raging in the United States; we are tentatively coming out of our homes and into public spaces in order to work and play and learn. There is much to rebuild: 2020 has disrupted almost every aspect of the economy. Moreover, we are still waiting on a full distribution of vaccines against the virus, and we will have to alter our interactions until it is complete.

Soon, my university will reopen, and I will go back to work. I am looking forward to being out among people, even at a distance. I am delighted that *The Story of More* is finding a new audience, as the future belongs to those young enough to shape it, hence this edition for a younger set of readers. If anything, I now believe even more strongly in the hopeful thesis of this book: that hidden inside humanity's capacity to make a problem is the capacity to solve it.

Like everyone I know, I hate and fear COVID-19 and wish it had never come upon us, but as the great Korean poet Yu Chi-hwan wrote, "Hope can flow even into a torn pocket"[1]. Even if greenhouse gases did not plunge as a side effect of the tragedy, we have learned something about *ourselves*. For the first time in at least a generation, we slowed to a stop, we let go, and we lived without. This makes us a people who can do so, when we have to. Whether it makes us a people who can commit to doing as much as it takes is a more difficult question, and we must find the answer together.

1   From the poem "Nostalgia" by Yu Chi-hwan

PART ONE

LIFE

The universe is change; our life is what our thoughts make it.

—MARCUS AURELIUS ANTONINUS (121–180 CE)

1

OUR STORY BEGINS

The sun and solar energy. What a source of
power! I hope we don't have to wait until oil and
coal run out before we tackle that.

—THOMAS EDISON TO HENRY FORD

AND HARVEY FIRESTONE (1931)

You have probably been hearing about climate change
your whole life. Maybe you've seen it on the news, or
seen movies about it, or read about it in school, or heard
people debating about it in your home. You've probably
heard people ask if climate change is real. Is it something
we should be afraid of? When will it happen and how
bad will it be? You may have heard it called a "hoax." You
may have heard it called "the biggest challenge your generation will ever face." You might even be sick of hearing
about it altogether.

You know what? I get it. I'm more than fifty years old,
and I've been hearing people argue over climate change
for at least twenty years. I am a scientist who studies
climate change, and so—lucky me—I get to hear people

argue about it almost every day. But lately I learned that the arguments go back much further than that.

In 1969, more than half a century ago, the Norwegian explorer Bernt Balchen noticed a thinning trend in the ice that covered the North Pole. He warned his colleagues that the Arctic Ocean was melting into an open sea. *The New York Times* picked up the story, and Walter Wittmann of the US Navy immediately disagreed: he had seen no evidence of thinning during his monthly airplane flights over the pole.

But that's not nearly all: in 1931, Thomas Edison said to Henry Ford and Harvey Firestone, "The sun and solar energy. What a source of power! I hope we don't have to wait until oil and coal run out before we tackle that." That's right—the guy who invented the light bulb (Edison) urged renewable energy on the guy who invented the car (Ford) and the guy who invented the tire (Firestone). Almost *one hundred years ago* these important men were talking about "green energy," while at the very same time, they were initiating our modern addiction to fossil fuels.

Let's go back to 1969 for a moment, back when Balchen was fighting with Wittmann. I don't remember 1969 personally, but, like every year, it was full of beginnings and endings, problems and solutions, equal to any that had gone before or have come since.

Most of the trees you see out your window were barely seeds in 1969. Wal-Mart Stores, Inc., was incorporated in 1969 and has since become the world's largest private employer. *Sesame Street* premiered in 1969 and went on to teach millions of children how to count and spell. Big things started out as small things, then grew to change the world.

Way up north, in Mower County, Minnesota, my parents weren't paying attention, for I was one of the ten million babies born on September 27, 1969, and the last of their four children. The world would be different for this baby, my parents promised each other, and they made the ancient vow that all mothers and fathers make in the euphoria that follows a happy birth.

I would have all the love that my father could give and all the love that my mother should have been given. She will grow up free, my mother resolved—free from hunger and from the shame of being taken by the county. My father, for his part, looked forward to a century of technologies that would save us all from sickness and want. Like the millions of couples who had come before them, and would come after, they looked at the world they lived in and thought about the one they wanted. Then my parents turned to each other, in love, and they named me Hope.

Forty years later, in 2009, my department chair called me into his office and asked me to teach a class on climate change. I'll admit that, at first, I was not excited about the idea. Convincing people to lower their energy use is like trying to get them to quit smoking or to eat more healthfully: they already suspect they should do it, but there's a billion-dollar industry working round the clock, inventing new ways to make sure they don't. I would start, I conceded, by taking my boss's orders at face value. I sat down at my desk, turned on my computer, and began to research *change*. Over the next several years, I cataloged the data that describes how population has increased, how agriculture has intensified, how energy use has skyrocketed over the last half century. I accessed public databases and downloaded files of numbers and spreadsheets. I searched through the data for patterns across the decades of my own life. I set out to quantify global change in the most concrete and precise terms that I could apprehend, and I learned a lot by doing it.

This research became the foundation of a course I taught many times. Each week during the semester, I'd pick up the chalk and teach a room full of students the numbers describing how planet Earth had changed since I was a kid back in the 1970s. I taught them what has happened. Not what I think *might* happen. Not what I think *should* happen. I taught them the things that I had taught myself. And as I did my job, I finally began to understand why I was doing it: because only after we see where we are can we duly ask ourselves if this is where we want to be. At the bottom of it all, I had learned, we have only four resources: the earth, the ocean, the sky, and each other.

All of this has convinced me that it's time to bring global change out of my classroom and into this book. Not because I am a scientist who thinks she's right, but because I am an author who loves both words and numbers, and a teacher who has something to say.

So if you'll listen, I'll tell you what happened to my world, to your world—to *our* world. It changed.

2

WHO WE ARE

Four thousand years ago, the people living along the Tigris-Euphrates River valley in a place they called Mesopotamia, were deeply worried that planet Earth could never provide enough food, water, shelter, and space for the population they saw increasing all around them. Their poets wrote about "the countless tribes of men" who "oppressed the surface of the deep-bosomed Earth." These poems were written in about 1800 BC, just as world population hit somewhere near one hundred million people. During the one thousand years that followed, global population doubled.

The famous Greek philosopher Aristotle believed that politicians should decide "of what numbers and of what sort of people" a country should contain because, according to him, "too large a multitude are incapable" of keeping themselves in good order. If people would just follow his directions, Aristotle insisted, the population would be appropriately curbed, and Earth would forever be able to supply its inhabitants with the "necessaries of life." He wrote these things over two thousand years ago, just as world population was nearing 250 million. During the one thousand years that followed, global population doubled again.

A priest named Suger spent much of his life raising funds to renovate his church entrance, which was so crowded that it "forced women to run to the altar on the heads of men as on a pavement" due to the population explosion of the High Middle Ages. Suger wrote this nine hundred years ago, when the world population was about one-half billion people. Within the next five hundred years, global population doubled yet again.

Thomas Robert Malthus made people really nervous in 1798, when he wrote *An Essay on the Principle of Population.* Any and every improvement in food production, he argued, would give rise to an increase in population that would, in turn, reestablish a state of want. Malthus believed that our planet writhes within an everlasting state of overpopulation and that every bite we put into our mouths makes things worse. When he published his essay, the world's population was approaching one billion, and during the one hundred years that followed, global population doubled again.

Fifty years later, a man named John Stuart Mill expanded Malthus's argument to include the broader economic "penalty attached to over-population." He spelled out his idea this way: "A greater number of people can not, in any given state of civilization, be collectively so well provided for as a smaller." John Stuart Mill insisted these things during 1848, just as world population approached 1.5 billion people. And within the next century, the global population doubled again.

There was another man who saw things differently: an American economist named Henry George. He believed in a hopeful feedback loop between human population and food production: "Give more food, open fuller conditions of life, and the vegetable or animal can but multiply; the man will develop."

Henry George was a humble and pious man; he had known poverty and lived modestly even after success. He was ahead of his time in many ways, advocating for public transportation, labor unions, and a half-female Congress during the nineteenth century, but the public loved him. More than a hundred thousand mourners attended his funeral after he died in 1897. It also turns out that Henry George, out of all those important men who came before him, was the one who came closest to being right about population growth.

The doubling of global population that has occurred since the time of Henry George was accompanied by a *tripling* of grain production, a *tripling* in fish production, and a *quadrupling* in meat production. The arrival of more people has indeed coincided with greater food production, just as Henry George believed it would—far above and beyond what was strictly required.

Henry George was also right in that most of the want and suffering we see in our world today originates not from Earth's inability to *provide* but from our inability to *share,* as we'll see so many times in later pages. It is because so many of us consume far beyond our needs that a great many more of us are left with almost nothing.

And what about *now*? What about *us*? As for me, I was born just over fifty years ago, in 1969, adding one small female to what was then a world population of 3.5 billion people. Between then and now—that is, over the course of my lifetime so far—the global population has doubled yet again.

Today, you and I share the world with more than seven billion people.

This means that, unless some terrible sickness or war

devastates not just countries but whole continents, our earth will never again contain fewer than seven billion people. We must learn to live together if we want to live well. How can we do this?

Ultimately, we are endowed with only four resources: the earth, the ocean, the sky, and each other.

Because absolutely everything is at stake, we should begin by thinking clearly and simply. Let's begin where every human story begins. We'll begin with a baby.

3

HOW WE ARE

It is difficult for us to imagine, but two hundred years ago, losing a child was very common. In 1819, two out of every five children born alive, the world over, died before their fifth birthday. Because family size was much larger than it is today—a woman of that time gave birth, on average, six times during her lifetime—it would have been rare to meet a family who had not endured this terrible grief at least once, if not twice. By the time I was born in 1969, survival was the norm. Any number is still too high, but during the last two hundred years, childhood deaths have been reduced drastically: at present, one out of twenty-five babies dies before they turn five. Because families are also smaller now (each woman gives birth, as a global average, about three times during her lifetime), we encounter this great loss and its devastation far less regularly, and the world is better for it.

Two hundred years ago, it was not only the baby that risked death while being born; the mother did as well. One hundred years ago, one out of every hundred live births in the United States resulted in a dead mother. Since then, improved medical care in the form of a midwife, a nurse, or a physician with access to sterile medical tools has greatly lessened the risk for both mother and baby during childbirth. These advances have brought the United States down to one maternal death for every ten thousand live births. Around the world, one in five hundred live births results in the death of the mother, a great decrease compared to just a few decades ago.

What will you do for fun when you are sixty-five years old? I hope to still be riding my bicycle regularly and picture myself coasting downhill through a light blizzard of cottonwood fluff during June 2034. I stop at dusk to lock up outside Target Field and take my seat just in time to see the Minnesota Twins win handily in eight and a half innings, 17–0 against the Yankees.

I have good reason to make such plans, though my father never did. When he was born in 1923, the life expectancy for a newborn American child was only fifty-eight years. When I was born almost five decades later, that number had increased such that I can expect to live to be seventy-one. My son must plan not only his sixties but his seventies as well: by the time he was born in 2004, American life expectancy had increased to seventy-eight years. I encourage him to plan beyond eighty, and not without cause, for my own father lived past his ninety-second birthday. He died of pneumonia, which is an infectious disease of the respiratory system, and while it is a common cause of death in ninety-plus-year-olds, it is otherwise a very unusual way to die in America.

My father could have been one of the more than four hundred thousand American men who died while fighting in World War II between the years 1939 and 1945, but he wasn't. Wars result in a terrible loss of life; the number of deaths around the globe each year due to wartime conflicts averages about fifty thousand people, as of the last few years. What police call "conventional homicide" continues to kill many more people than war does: five hundred thousand murders occur each year around the globe. But murder and war, even when added together, pale in comparison with the annual loss of life due to suicide: our world witnessed almost eight hundred thousand suicides during 2016, fifty thousand of them occurring in America. For all the violence we perpetrate against one another, we inflict much more upon ourselves.

The vast majority of human deaths that occur on planet Earth each year, however, are due simply to illness.

The year 2020 was an unusual and awful year. Summed all together, almost two million people died of the viral illness COVID-19. Many of these deaths were people who would have otherwise lived through the year. Now, in just the first five months of 2021, COVID-19 has wrought almost as many deaths as it did during the whole of 2020, and we see the tragedy increasing. Scientists will be studying the effect of COVID-19 on both humans and the environment for many years to come. Right now, the most urgent priority is to decrease the death toll of this terrible pandemic.

For the five more normal years before COVID-19, about 1 percent of the population became sick and died each year, of predictable causes; in 2019, that amounted to something like fifty-seven million people. In the richer countries, the top two killers are heart disease and stroke, which account for one out of every four deaths. Taken together with cancer, diabetes, and kidney disease, they are responsible for about half of all deaths within the world's wealthiest nations. Each of these diseases is dreadful in its own way, but they have something important in common: none of them are contagious.

Within the poorest regions of the world, the story is very different. People may be dying at the same rate, but they suffer and expire at a younger age and from diseases that have been almost eliminated within richer countries through access to clean water, improved sewage systems, vaccination, and antibiotics. Contagious infections of the lungs, intestines, and blood are responsible for 30 percent of the deaths in the poorest regions of the world, and tragedy during childbirth accounts for another 10 percent.

Nevertheless, being poor on planet Earth does not carry the death sentence that it once did. During the last twenty-five years, access to clean water has increased by 30 percent and access to improved sanitation has doubled in the poorest nations of the world. Just in the last thirty years, rates of immunization have doubled and access to medical care during pregnancy has increased by more than 30 percent in those regions. The result is that the death rate in poor nations is now less than half of what it was when I was born in 1969, and as I mentioned above, it is now equal to what it is in wealthier nations.

How, exactly, during the last fifty years did so much more of the world come to better fight disease and survive childbirth? They mostly did it the same way my grandparents did it a hundred years ago: by packing up and moving into town.

4

WHERE WE ARE

How many generations must you trace back in order to encounter a farmer? In my case, I need look only to my mother's parents, both of whom grew up on the pastures of southern Minnesota and northern Iowa. My grandfather, after returning from World War I, wandered the country at loose ends until he met my grandmother. They got married and had children—one of whom grew up to become my mother. In 1920, town life called and they answered: my grandparents permanently relocated their young family to my hometown of Austin, Minnesota, and my grandfather took up indoors work in the hog kill.

If you must look back more than nine generations to find a farmer, or a rancher, or a trapper, then your family history is extremely unusual. In 1817, only 3 percent of the global population lived in any kind of city. Now, just two hundred years later, about half the people on planet Earth reside in cities—that is, within urban centers containing at least one hundred thousand people. Cities may hold half the world's population, but they are also distributed very unevenly around the globe.

Understanding where people are is fairly straightforward. The "highly developed" set of countries, which include the European Union, the United Kingdom, North America, Japan, Israel, New Zealand, and Australia (sometimes known as the Organisation for Economic Cooperation and Development, or OECD), all put together add up to just over one billion people. Amazingly, there are now two countries in the world that can boast more than one billion citizens: China and India each contains about one and a half billion people. The portion of Africa that sits south of the Sahara Desert is also home to about one billion people. Similarly, the countries of East Asia (not including China) add up to about a billion people. The Arab countries of North Africa and the Middle East are home to half a billion people—as are Latin America and the rest of South Asia (not including India). The exact total, as of 2017, came to seven and a half billion people on planet Earth.

Cities are the very definition of *more*—hot spots of humanity visible from space. At night, they pulse with artificial light, and from above, they resemble nothing so much as the network of nerves in the brain. Lots of people translate into the possibility of lots of activity: Henry George was right, back in 1881, when he wrote that as new people arrive, "the hands they bring with them can in the natural order of things produce *more.*" The history of cities reveals libraries, construction projects, transportation systems, bazaars, hospitals, bureaucracies, judiciaries, and other enterprises that could never have been accomplished in low-density population settings. Cities always have been, and always will be, places where people come together in an attempt to divide and multiply their labor.

For my part, I was born and grew up in the same small town where my grandparents had landed in 1920 (pop. 10,000). When I became an adult, I moved to an urban area with a population of more than one million, seeking education and work—a very common story the world over. During the last half century, just over one billion people either moved into or were born into a city that already contained more than one million people. I was one of the many who migrated into the city, and we all did it for more or less the same reason: in hopes of finding opportunities that we did not see at home.

The world's cities will continue to grow; on every inhabited continent, people are migrating from rural areas into cities. Even in places such as Europe and North America, where more than 80 percent of the population already lives in cities, people are still migrating away from the country. And don't forget that total global population is still increasing as well; a realistic estimate is that we'll break the ten-billion mark by 2100. More people in more cities require more *more* in general, but especially food.

Which begs a question: After the whole world moves to the city, who is left to run the farms? The answer: Almost nobody. And the almost nobody who currently grows the food that is keeping you and me alive is what we will talk about next.

PART TWO

FOOD

The world moves on with giant strides,
Last year abundance, famine this;
You see to what a monstrous girth
The folks' necessities have swell'd.

—HENRIK IBSEN, *BRAND* (1865)

5

GROWING GRAIN

Where are you from? I'm not asking where you were born, but rather, where you made your first memories. What was the first landscape you remember seeing out the car window? Desert? Ocean? Plains? Mountains? Trees? Buildings? I remember being very little, staring out the car window, and watching farm fields go by.

In November, the fields were barren, their black soil powdered with frost. After winter descended, everything went white, and I was unable to pick out the horizon from the colorless expanse that surrounded us. In April, all that snow turned to slush in one day, and meltwater streamed through the ditches on both sides. During May, I cracked my window to smell the thick air of planting as giant mechanical cultivators groomed the fields into rows. Plowing back and forth at six miles per hour, they looked like solitary metal beasts pacing their territory and marking the path behind them.

By the first of June, the corn was seeded and the soybeans were in the ground. Springtime rains never failed, and soon, tiny green blades of corn bristled up in rows. When pea-green ovals popped up one week later, we knew the beans had taken. Then summer subsumed everything, and the crops rose up—inch by inch, foot by foot—regreening the world around us.

Corn and soybeans are strange associates, often found right next to each other but different to their core. Soybeans are harder to *not* grow than to grow: they get their nutrients from the bacteria trapped in their roots, while corn plants require lavish applications of fertilizer. Soybean flowers are self-pollinating and so develop embryos without help, while every single seed on a corncob must be pollinated individually. Soybeans are harvested from a pod, four seedy knuckles inside a green leather glove. Corn embryos harden and dry by the hundreds, lining the cobs that hang from a stalk. Once corn and soybeans are fully mature, however, they meet the same end, both of them destined for the silo.

In October, the tractors reappeared, this time dragging behemoth combines that gathered all and left nothing in their wake. By Halloween, the entire county was a carpet of uneven stubble, and the odd dry husk whipping about was the only evidence of summer's bursting glory. By November, the first frost had come, and the cycle had started all over again.

The portion of America that stretches east to west from Chicago to Cheyenne and north to south from Fargo to Wichita is sometimes known as the "heartland." While the heartland makes up only 15 percent of the land area of the United States, it is home to more than half its farm fields. Austin, Minnesota, where I grew up, is near the center, in the very heart of the heartland.

Austin has a big factory and a few small restaurants, mostly diners and fast-food places. Unlike much of small-town America, my hometown is not a ghost town: it has thrived in its own little way. It is a few hundred buildings surrounded by an ocean of soybeans, alfalfa, and corn. Until I was seventeen, that square mile of town and the farm fields at its edges was the whole universe to me. But it turns out that much of what I saw happening in the farm fields of Mower County—barren, blooming, and bursting by turn—was also representative of what was happening the world over.

Today, the farm fields of my home county produce over three times more food than they did when I was born in 1969. Likewise, the farm fields of planet Earth produce three times more food than they did in 1969. A planet that once produced one billion tons of cereal each year now produces three billion tons. More amazing still is that the amount of land being farmed has not much increased in America over that same time period, nor has it much increased worldwide.

How did we come to be growing three times more food on only 10 percent more land? The answer has to do with gigantic increases in *yield*—the amount of grain produced per footprint of soil.

A bushel is a unit of measurement that has been in use for more than a thousand years. One bushel of crop fills a basket that would hold just over eight gallons of fluid; it's a lot to carry, but not impossible. A bushel of grain weighs fifty to sixty pounds, which is a bit over the maximum that you are allowed to check in your suitcase when riding on an airplane. Fifty years ago, a plot of land the size of a basketball court was required to produce one bushel of corn; today, all that is needed is two parking spaces.

Both wheat and rice show the same stunning increase as corn, their average yields more than doubling over the last fifty years. Soybeans, barley, oats, rye, and millet all show dramatic increases as well. Not only that, but coffee, tobacco, and sugar-beet yields have increased by more than 50 percent—in fact, every single crop I researched for this book showed a big increase in yield over the last half century.

With very, very few exceptions, every farm field on planet Earth produces *at least* twice as much food today compared with fifty years ago, and it's a good thing too, as the planet contains twice as many people today compared to fifty years ago. This amazing agricultural feat was actually the result of three separate but related accomplishments: we feed plants better now than we did then, we protect them better, and we have improved the plants themselves.

Every plant on Earth—including a tomato bush, a beanstalk, or a tuft of wheat—needs water and nutrients to survive and grow. A plant can get these things from only one place: the soil beneath it, a complex mixture of dead leaves and degraded rock that has rotted belowground for hundreds, if not thousands, of years.

Different types of plants have different nutritional needs, and every handful of soil contains a unique combination of offerings. Variation in the amount of nutrition available to plants, coupled with the differing nutritional needs of different types of plants, is what gives rise to different ecosystems; grassland *versus* rain forest *versus* wetland, for example. In contrast, a farm field is a completely artificial landscape; it must support a "monoculture," one single, designated plant type. The soil of a farm field is forced to be the perfect environment for that one plant's growth. This is achieved by adding nutrients in the form of fertilizer and water through irrigation. During the last fifty years, engineers and crop scientists have helped farmers develop better and better methods for supplying exactly the right amount of both.

World use of fertilizer has tripled since 1969, and the global capacity for irrigation has almost doubled; we are feeding and watering our fields more lavishly than ever, and our crops are loving it. Unfortunately, these luxurious conditions have also excited the attention of weeds and pests.

Because farm fields are loaded with nutrients and water relative to the natural land that surrounds them, they are considered luxury real estate by every random weed in the county. In addition, the fields that were plowed for planting were already home to insects, fungi, and bacteria that are only too eager to eat key parts of our crop plants before we can. To control these pests, farmers use "pesticides," chemicals that are poisonous to the weeds, insects, and microorganisms that would otherwise eat away at the monoculture—and are sometimes toxic to human beings as well.

Today, more than five million tons of pesticides are applied to cropland each year the world over—that's a little more than one pound for every person on Earth, and it represents a tripling in the manufacture of pesticides since 1969. Different crops require different poisons: the greenhouses of the tropics are fogged with tons of a chemical called "chlorothalonil" to keep strawberries from molding; the rice paddies of China, Japan, and Korea are sprayed with thousands of tons of "chloropyrifos" to keep insects from breeding; millions of acres are soaked in "atrazine" to keep weeds from invading the vast croplands of the middle latitudes; and fertilizer is slathered just about everywhere. Thanks to this, our farm fields are the ultimate safe spaces for the plants that we choose to grow and harvest. Our crops grow tall and strong, oblivious to all the weeds that would steal their precious sun and immune to all the beings that would eat them who are not us.

But even more important, and harder to explain, is how the corn, soybeans, wheat, and rice that we grow today are not the corn, soybeans, wheat, and rice of fifty years ago: they are, in fact, better versions of themselves.

The edible portion of a crop plant is an exaggerated feature—it is a fruit, seed, stem, or root that is loaded with sugars, oils, and proteins and bloated in size compared with its wild ancestor. Have you ever picked wild blueberries, dug for wild potatoes, or plucked wild grapes? They are significantly smaller, and often less sweet, than their grocery store counterparts. The same is true for the grassy ancestors of wheat, rice, corn, and other grains; thousands of years of deliberate selection of the plants with the biggest, juiciest kernels was performed by our great-great-great-and-more-grandparents. This process is called "domestication" and it describes how nutritious grains, fruits, and vegetables may be bred from their wild ancestors.

The ancient practice of plant breeding sped up during the early nineteen hundreds, after scientists improved the rules of crossbreeding that the famous monk Gregor Mendel came up with by growing yellow and green, round and shriveled peas in his monastery's garden. Within the research fields and greenhouses of the 1920s and 1930s, scientists purposefully mated individual crop plants and kept careful records of the offspring. They created "hybrids" by mating these offspring to each other and encountered unusual variations from the results. For more than five decades, scientists "genetically modified" all of the major grains grown on Earth, as well as most of the fruits and vegetables, using only a basic picture of plant breeding as their guide. The effect was amazing: grain yields tripled between 1900 and 1990, but more breakthroughs were still to come.

DNA—deoxyribonucleic acid—is a chemical that is present in every living cell. The molecule itself is shaped like a twisted chain and made of individual links. Only a handful of different links exists in nature, and yet every individual—each mushroom, human, palm tree—

contains a completely unique sequence of a couple of dozen links. The key to this uniqueness is the total length of each chain—fungus DNA is a chain with millions of links, human DNA contains billions of links, and plant DNA can approach a trillion links.

Morse code is made of just two types of signals, which sound like long and short beeps to the human ear. Written out, a chain made of Morse code "dot" and "dash" links can communicate everything from a simple SOS distress call to all five acts of Shakespeare's *Hamlet*. In a similar way, biological DNA codes—not for words but for proteins—make up one long recipe book. We refer to the individual recipes as "genes": a subchain of links that describes how to make a useful protein. Every gene is a recipe for a protein, and every protein is capable of doing a job—some of them very important jobs.

During reproduction, the DNA chain from your biological mother was patched together with the DNA chain from your biological father to form a new DNA chain that's part one, part the other. From this, you formed! Your DNA codes for a collection of genes that is not identical to that of either of your biological parents: you kept some protein recipes from each parent and lost others. Breeding new crops also involves reproduction: the crop scientists of the early twentieth century mated plant-parents that possessed desirable qualities, hoping to concentrate those qualities in the offspring, and it worked wonderfully, even if they couldn't spell out exactly which proteins in the DNA chain had been kept or lost.

One of the biggest breakthroughs of the twentieth century was a new method that allowed scientists to map out an entire chain of DNA, link by link. They called this new field "molecular genetics," and it allowed scientists to pinpoint individual genes within DNA chains that were thousands, millions, billions of links long. Then, in the 1980s, they perfected a new method to alter DNA—a method that didn't require the hassle of breeding parents and waiting for a new generation to mature. These new "recombinant" technologies allowed geneticists to directly edit the sequence of links in DNA: they could delete, copy, and paste genes, all within the DNA chain of a living plant, sort of like how we delete, copy, and paste words in and out of a very long sentence. Scientists could even cut genes from nonplant DNA and paste them into plant DNA, infusing a baby plant with recipes for proteins that it would never have figured out how to make otherwise.

The group of crops that resulted from these recombinant methods is known as "GMOs" ("genetically modified organisms" or, more rarely, "transgenics"). GMO grains are just as nutritious as their non-GMO (sometimes called "conventional" or "nontransgenic") parents, but they also contain recipes for proteins that make them less water-demanding and more resistant to pests than their ancestors. GMO plants are simply better versions of their parents, who were, in turn, better versions of their parents; the only difference is that this newest generation was engineered directly from its own DNA.

The fact that GMO plants have laboratory-altered DNA does not make them dangerous for human consumption; the National Academy of Sciences has formally reviewed the safety of GMO crops twice now and found that they pose no hazard to human health. Today, just thirty years after their introduction, a full 10 percent of the world's croplands are planted with GMO crops. Almost all the soybeans, corn, cotton, and canola growing in the United States are now GMO varieties: all of them were invented after I was born.

Much of the exploding green that I observed from my car window in Minnesota owed itself to the adoption of GMO soybeans and GMO corn within fields that had previously been planted with conventional varieties. After the introduction of these GMO crops during the 1990s, the global yields of corn and soybeans increased by at least *another* 30 percent and are now more than quadruple what they were at the beginning of the twentieth century.

* * *

Somehow, whenever I talk about farming, all roads lead to the state of Iowa. It's not just that I grew up in a small town where most of the roads did, in fact, lead to Iowa. It's also because the state of Iowa has always done the heavy lifting for agricultural America. There were years during my childhood in the 1970s when Iowa came close to producing one-quarter of the country's number one crop. The state of Iowa always has been, and probably always will be, the most productive farm field in the world.

When I was in high school, more than 80 percent of Iowa was farmland. And today, thirty years later, more than 80 percent of Iowa is farmland. Iowa has never *not* been more than 80 percent farmland.

But back in the 1970s, Iowa's farmland had almost twice as many individual farms as there are now; since then, land was bought and sold such that most farms got smaller and smaller, while a few farms accumulated land to become huge. Today, the largest farms in Iowa are twice as big as New York City and harvest more than a million bushels of corn every single year.

Today, there are just under ninety thousand farmers in all of Iowa (they are designated as "agricultural principal operators" in the census). This amounts to just 3 percent of the state population being responsible for nearly 10 percent of the state's economy. Farming is an important job, but very few people do it.

*   *   *

One fact that may shock you is that most of the grain we grow in America's heartland is never eaten by people. Take corn, for example. The United States has always been a garden of corn. In 1870, five years after the end of the Civil War, when all was chaos, America still managed to produce one billion bushels of corn. By 1890, production was back up to two billion bushels each year. During the economic boom that followed World War II, corn harvests approached three billion bushels.

By the time I was a child in the 1970s, America was regularly producing five billion bushels of corn every year—more than all its other major grains combined. Today, annual corn production in the United States is at fifteen billion bushels—a stunning 300 percent increase over the past fifty years.

This massive stockpiling of American corn has encouraged the development of new and unusual industries dedicated to getting rid of corn. We eat processed corn not only as cornmeal but also in forms as varied as gum, acid, wax, and MSG (monosodium glutamate), as well as the more recognizable starches, sugars, and oil. Nevertheless, human consumption of corn uses up only 10 percent of the US annual harvest. Where does the rest of it go?

Half of the remainder (that is, 45 percent of the corn that will be planted, fertilized, and harvested this year) will never be used as food, as we'll see in Chapter 12. Out of that other half, more than one billion bushels—enough to feed one hundred million people for an entire year—will be eaten by animals, and ultimately converted directly into manure.

6

RAISING MEAT

Once upon a time, in Ukraine, there lived a cow. To be more accurate, it was a steer—a male bovine that had been castrated just after weaning. The steer was young and strong and beautiful and had many admirers. My friend was one of them.

My friend is a journalist and she was traveling in eastern Europe, writing about important events in the local women's lives. Her tour guide for that day was a man preparing for his sister's upcoming wedding. He drove my friend through a sunny, green valley and stopped the car next to a small holding pen that had been carefully constructed and decorated. In the middle of the enclosure stood a lone steer, chewing contentedly.

"This is the cow that I will slaughter for the wedding," the man said proudly, beaming toward the healthy animal. He explained how everyone in the village would be invited to the celebration. Each guest would prepare her very best dish for the party, but the animal standing before them was destined to become the crowning glory of the feast.

My friend looked at the docile animal and thought of its death. The steer looked back at her for a moment, then lowered its head, deeply inhaled the earth beneath its feet, and took another bite of grass.

In America, by contrast, it is very unusual for a person to meet her meat, even though on average she eats ten food items derived from meat every single day. It is also not unusual for the meat she eats each day to have come from the bodies of at least ten different animals. About one million animals are slaughtered for food every hour in the United States. This slaughter mostly takes place within airport-sized buildings, and huge swaths of the country specialize in different types of killing. Thirty million cattle are slaughtered each year in the Great Plains of Nebraska, Colorado, and Kansas. A whopping nine billion chickens are slaughtered each year across the Feather Belt, which stretches from Arkansas to Georgia. One hundred and twenty million pigs are slaughtered each year in the Upper Midwest states that surround Iowa.

The biggest industry in Austin, Minnesota, is a giant hog kill: fully 6 percent of the hogs slaughtered in the United States each year breathe their last within the city limits of my tiny hometown. Between Fourth and Eighth Streets Northeast, thirteen hundred people kill nineteen thousand hogs every single day. Most of the meat is made into the product Spam. Spam was *invented* in my hometown in 1937 but has become world-famous since then: it is now eaten in eighty different countries at a global rate of one can every seventy-eight milliseconds.

Since 2011, global production of meat has exceeded three hundred million tons per year—this is three times the amount that was produced fifty years ago. Almost all of this meat (97 percent) comes from just three pitiable animals: cattle, chickens, and pigs—the same three that made up almost 90 percent of our meat fifty years ago. Some important things have changed, however, in that we now can get much more meat from an individual animal. To get twice as much beef, we slaughter only half again as many cattle as we did in 1969; to get four times more pork, we butcher only three times more pigs; to get ten times more chicken meat, we slaughter only six times more chickens.

The trend holds true for other animal products too. The world's hens now lay more than a trillion eggs each year—that's quadruple the production of 1969. Milk is a particularly shocking example: the United States produces twice as much milk as it did in 1969, but we get it from three million fewer cows. What's going on?

The answer has to do with *yield,* and it's not dissimilar to the explanation for how we are able to grow three times more grain on only 10 percent more land. We feed animals better now than we did then, we protect them better, and we have also improved the animals themselves.

Veterinary medicine, advancing through research, has brought new cures for animal disease and a better understanding of animal nutrition to the task of producing meat for market. More amazing still are the changes in animal bodies from seven decades of controlled breeding programs by agricultural researchers. Thanks to the work of a few thousand dedicated scientists, every single cow, pig, and chicken slaughtered worldwide is, on average, between 20 and 40 percent bigger than it was in 1969. More meat from less biology is the unlikely prize won from changing the biology of an animal to combine quick maturation, high fertility, and low metabolism.

During the 1950s, a calf commonly passed the one-hundred-pound mark during its third month of life; today, calves routinely break two hundred pounds in just fifty days. Today's milk cow produces more than six gallons of milk each day, which is double the amount of fifty years ago. In addition, mother pigs have a tougher job than they used to: in 1942, the average number of piglets weaned from a litter was five; today, it's ten—on top of this comes the fact that sows now have babies not once but twice a year. And as for the humble roasting chicken, he is a fundamentally different being to what he was sixty years ago: the amount of feed required to keep a two-pound chicken alive in 1957 is the same amount that keeps a ten-pound chicken alive today.

It took me some time to convince my journalist friend that when her Ukrainian host stopped his car beside that paddock, he wasn't doing it to show her an animal. He was showing her three years of hard work.

There's no such thing as a low-maintenance farm. A healthy steer, ready for slaughter, first grew inside a mother cow that required extra feed and tending for the 280 days of her pregnancy. After the calf was born, it required neutering, and after that came eighteen months of hauling hay, shoveling manure, moving pasture, fixing fences, watering, deworming, and—at the end—fattening. When my friend's guide chose his sister's wedding feast as the destination for all that meat, he was also gifting her the years of labor that he had performed to bring that steer up to the knife.

The production of meat requires an investment of resources; it is a process of concentrating a very large amount of raw materials into a relatively tiny product.

A full 30 percent of the fresh water used by humans on planet Earth is spent in the production, maintenance, and slaughter of meat animals. The twenty-five billion cows, pigs, and chickens that live in captivity while waiting to be slaughtered are also given medicine in vast amounts. As of 1990, two-thirds of the antibiotics used in the United States are fed to meat animals, supposedly to promote growth and health, though studies have shown that they don't work for either.

Most of these medicines pass through the animals, mixing with their urine and then into the runoff that floods the roadside ditches and seeps down into the groundwater. There, microorganisms strive to breed strains that can successfully resist the antibiotics and make our medicines less effective in the long run.

The main thing you must pump into an animal to produce meat, however, is grain—a mountain of grain. More than sixty billion bushels of grain—mostly corn, soybeans, and wheat—are fed to meat animals every single year. When an animal eats grain, its body uses the grain for many things, but mostly not to build flesh.

Whenever a farm animal moves, every muscle that contracts uses energy gained from burning the food it ate. Therefore, if animals move less, they require less food overall: this has given rise to cages so confining that the animal within may not even be able to turn its head from side to side. Even inside these contraptions, six pounds of grain fed to an animal results in only one pound of meat that can be harvested, as a rule.

In the world today, a billion tons of grain are eaten by humans while, at the same time, a different billion tons of grain are offered to animals as feed. From all this feed, we get about one hundred million tons of meat and three hundred million tons of animal feces.

As a species, human beings will slaughter six times more animals for their meat this year than they did back in 1969, and a full 10 percent of this killing will take place in the United States. Probably you know people who have strong ideas about whether this killing is right or wrong. Perhaps you have friends or family members who describe themselves as "vegetarian," "vegan," "pescatarian," or "omnivorous"—terms meant to reflect the degree to which animals are included versus excluded in their diet. However, these labels do not capture one very important lifestyle: the middle ground, where we would still eat meat, but we would eat much less of it than we do now.

If every American cut their red meat and poultry intake by half—down from four to two pounds a week—it would free up 150 million tons of feed, of edible grain that could be used for purposes other than raising meat. It would not be much of a sacrifice: two pounds of meat per week per person is generous compared with the consumption in many countries—it is still higher than the average consumption in Ukraine, for example. And the freed-up grain would increase the world's food-grain supply by 15 percent, which is quite a lot!

If the thirty-six countries of the OECD (essentially North America, United Kingdom, Europe, Israel, Australia, New Zealand, and Japan) together decreased their meat consumption by half, the world's food-grain supply would get bumped up by almost 40 percent. Or to put it another way: if the entire OECD adopted the habit of just one meatless day per week, an extra 120 million tons of grain would be available to feed the hungry this very year.

How many hungry people are there on planet Earth? For more than eight hundred million children, women, and men, daily food intake falls "below the minimum level of dietary energy consumption needed to support the activities of life"; in other words, we share the earth with eight hundred million people who are starving.

There is absolutely no reason why anyone should have to live—or die—this way. *Starvation is caused by our failure to share what we produce, not by the earth's ability to provide.* Even with meat production gobbling up one-third of the world's edible grain supply, the world still produces, overall, enough calories to support the energy requirements for a healthy life for every person. Because so many countries consume so much more food than we need, many, many others are left with far too little.

The most cautious predictions of global population put the world's total inhabitants near ten billion by the year 2100—that's an additional two and a half billion people compared to today. This means that you, and I, and the rest of the world have a little more than eight decades to figure out how to add another two quadrillion calories to the annual food supply—and to share it out—to avoid widespread starvation.

Humanity has been in this exact jam before, back in 1950 when it became clear that the global population would exceed four billion, and we wriggled out of it by increasing yields. But we've already played that ace. There is only so much corn that can be hung from a stalk and only so much meat that can be balanced on a backbone—we are running up against the biological limits of what our food can be. Sooner or later we will have to reconsider the fact that every year, we actively waste 90 percent of the grain we feed to animals, in exchange for a little meat and a lot of manure.

So much about the future is uncertain, but the fact that we need to eat will never go away. The total number of people is increasing, and we need to figure out sooner rather than later how we might feed them all. At present, we are choosing ourselves over our future three times a day, when we ignore the problem, pick up our forks, and take another bite of meat.

7

Finding Fish

Norway is the happiest country in the world, according to every major news outlet in 2017, which is something to remind yourself of when you're sitting outside on a frozen bench, watching the guy on the other side of the train tracks pick bits of herring out of his beard and eat them. It is a country of five million people—that's smaller than the population of metropolitan Atlanta—and when I'm not waiting in the cold for a late train, I admit that I'm pretty happy living here as well.

Norway is a wealthy country, thanks to the discovery of oil bordering its western coast, underlying the North Sea. Millions of years before Norway began harvesting fossil fuel from the ocean floor, however, the waters that surrounded the land roiled with a different kind of export gold.

The North Sea teems with fat philandering fish; it does now and it always has. Norwegians are also nothing short of amazing when it comes to finding those fish and hauling them home. Twelve thousand Norwegian men and women currently consider themselves full-time fishers, and they bring in almost 3 percent of the global annual catch. That's an average of more than two hundred tons of fish by each Norwegian fisher every single year. About thirty years ago, however, the Norwegian fishing industry became a whole new kind of amazing when it turned most of its efforts toward salmon and today, just seven thousand people supply the entire continent of Europe with its most popular fish.

It would be difficult to overstate the importance of salmon on Norwegian culture. *Salmo salar* (known as simply *laks* in Norwegian) is a hard-traveling fish. Hatched in fresh water, it feeds on insects and their larvae, an avid hunter from day one. As an adult, it roams the North Sea, tracking squid, eel, shrimp, and herring, eating and growing into a giant that can measure three feet in length and a hundred pounds in weight. Later in life, it struggles upriver, against the current, and returns to its freshwater origins to spawn a new generation.

Salmon flesh is stained with the rosy pigment of its conquered prey. It has been devoured by Nordic people for millennia—raw, cooked, smoked, pickled, or dug into the earth by handfuls and left to ferment. Where salmon go, Norwegians follow. The old Norse sagas, one thousand years old, tell how Grettir the Outlaw miraculously navigated his ship through the dangerous waters of western Iceland. Eventually, Grettir wandered into a tranquil fjord, where two rivers shared one mouth and emptied themselves into the salty sea, and noted a multitude of fat, jolly salmon striving upriver to spawn. He named the place Asgard, convinced that his gods had summoned him into their home. It was this sweet, sheltered valley—its icy streams writhing with salmon—that he believed to be the geographic location of Heaven.

Today, 99.99 percent of Norway's Atlantic salmon comes from places less sublime than Asgard, but on the other hand, there is now a truly otherworldly number of this fish. If you required the citizens of Norway to eat their country's entire annual production of salmon, you'd be forcing each woman, man, and child to ingest a pound and a half of salmon every day. Instead, more than 90 percent of the salmon produced in Norway is exported, mostly to the European Union and particularly to France. Even so, the per capita consumption of salmon in Norway is high—one hundred times higher than in the United States, for example. Salmon is everywhere in Norway: it's the cheapest fish you can buy in the grocery store. But it didn't use to be that way.

When I was a kid in the 1970s, the global annual production of Atlantic salmon was consistently about thirteen thousand tons per year. Today, global production is getting close to three million tons—which means that production has increased by more than 20,000 percent. When I was growing up, salmon was a fancy-dancy meal compared with cod or pollack or almost any whitefish. My relatives didn't serve salmon very often, and when they did, we had to eat all of it—even the skin (yuck). Nowadays, you can buy salmon at McDonald's (at least in Singapore). What happened?

The short answer is that Atlantic salmon no longer comes from the sea. Fifty years ago, the world's fishing boats went out each year and pulled thirteen thousand tons of salmon out of the ocean. Starting in 1990, that figure began to drop, until this year only about two thousand tons of salmon will be fished from the ocean.

Ocean fishing takes time and fuel, and risks damage to expensive boats, or even loss of life. What if, people asked, instead of searching the North Sea and catching only a *Salmo salar*, we simply collect the eggs and put them in a cage, grow the hatchlings into fish, then reach in and pull out a full-grown salmon whenever we feel like it? Similar questions were being asked all over the world for all kinds of seafood—not just fish but oysters, squid, crab, shrimp, and lobster too. Why not grow these creatures in a cage, or a pen, or a net, or a lagoon, and farm them in place instead of chasing them all over the ocean? And so an industry called "aquaculture" was born.

In 1969, when I was still a baby, brothers Ove and Sivert Grøntvedt put twenty thousand baby salmon into a net near the island of Hitra on the western coast of Norway, and the salmon did just fine. In fact, within the calm waters of the fjord, they thrived. The brothers pulled the net in, sold the salmon, and made a profit that very first year.

By 1990, there were easily one hundred times more *Salmo salar* living inside floating cages in Norwegian fjords than were being fished out of the ocean during an entire year. Just five years later, Norwegian aquaculture doubled its production of salmon, and by 2000, it doubled yet again.

Farming all those salmon in cages, nets, and pens has a cost, however. Traditional boat fishing is better in some ways: the fish live independently in the ocean until you catch them; this means they breed themselves, feed themselves, and succeed or fail as adults based upon their own efforts. When you raise salmon in a pen, you must hatch them, feed them, bathe them, vaccinate them, medicate them, examine them, and then tag them so you can move them from place to place. You also have to clean tons of feces out of the water, because fish excrete five times more than humans do, pound for pound.

Prior to 1990, global capture of wild seafood was actually increasing: between 1969 and 1990, it nearly doubled.

Most of this total was cod and pollack from the bottom waters, and tuna, mackerel, and herring from farther up. Many nations were noting a decline in wild fish populations as a result, so the idea of aquaculture seemed like a good one: a new source of dietary protein that could feed the increasing population while easing the pressure on natural populations of fish living in the ocean.

Thus 1990 marked a major shift in fishing all around the globe, not just in Norway. Between 1990 and today, global seafood production doubled, while the amount of fish pulled from the ocean did not change. This means that more than half of the fish eaten worldwide is now produced using aquaculture. Aquaculture is an important part of the increase in our ability to produce food during the last fifty years: the story of fish is similar to the stories of crop and meat production that we saw in chapters 5 and 6.

In 1969, the people of planet Earth ate about forty million tons of seafood, almost all of it as fish. Today, the total amount of seafood eaten each year is three times higher, but today, we commonly eat shrimp, crab, oysters, and other foods that were considered delicacies fifty years ago. The majority of all this seafood comes from aquaculture; massive scallop pens sprawl across the mudflats of the East China Sea, and a countless number of prawns ripen within the walled estuaries of Indonesia.

This great change in where we get seafood has not

only changed what we can eat from the ocean, it also threatens to change what can live in the ocean. Fish require food that is very high in protein, compared with animals that live on land. To supply this protein, aquaculture facilities use a feed made from small fish that have been ground into meal. All these small fish are taken out of the open ocean.

To get one pound of salmon, you need three pounds of fish meal. To get a pound of fish meal, you need to grind up five pounds of fish. Thus, each pound of cage-raised salmon "costs" fifteen pounds of fish from the ocean. At present, about one-third of all fish taken from the ocean (mostly small fish such as anchovies, herring, and sardines) is ground up into fish meal and then fed to the big fish that live in pens. When small fish are taken from the ocean for use in aquaculture, it means less food left in the ocean to feed sea animals like dolphins, sea lions, and humpback whales.

The story of aquaculture is simply that of meat production, only underwater. As such, it echoes the story of meat production on land: the rerouting of massive resources through small spaces that confine millions of animals who live short lives that end in our bellies. And, as with meat, every bite of fish that we do not take could free up many bites of food for someone else.

* * *

The last fifty years have also taught us that a fish cage isn't the only thing you can tie to the bottom of the ocean.

To be specific, you can tie a cutting of seaweed—green, red, or brown—and it will cheerfully grow into double, triple, or quadruple its original size, after which you may harvest as much as you wish and start the whole process over again. There are thousands of acres of such floating forests off the coast of China, and though they are home to no birds' nests, they sway in the gentle breeze of the current and dapple the light beneath their canopy.

Seaweed has been on dinner plates in Japan, China, and Korea for more than a thousand years, especially *Laminaria*—better known as kombu—a brown seaweed, and *Porphyra*—better known as nori—a red seaweed that dries to glossy black. Yet another result of the boom in shrimp, crab, tuna, and salmon brought about by aquaculture is that nori is now recognized around the world as the shiny dark ribbon that holds sushi together.

The global increase in seaweed production due to the development of aquaculture during the last fifty years is even more spectacular than that for fish. In 1969, just under two million tons of seaweed were harvested and marketed from the world's oceans; today, that number is closer to twenty-five million tons.

About half the global annual seaweed harvest is not eaten by people. It is dried, ground, and used as fertilizer for crops on land; another portion is used in feed for animals; and the remainder is processed into chemical additives for cosmetics, moisturizers, shampoos, tooth-pastes, lubricants, inks, and bandages and many other products. The other half of the global annual seaweed harvest is eaten by people, but not in any form we would recognize as seaweed.

Seaweed is made of very large molecules that can dis-solve into water to make a thick, slurpy solution. There are three main types: alginate, agar, and carrageenan. All three are low-calorie carbohydrates that can be used to thicken almost any solution. Today, when we purchase ice cream, whipped cream, and salad dressing, they were often made using recipes containing seaweed instead of milk, eggs, and cream.

Seaweed molecules are partly responsible for some-thing that is everywhere now but used to be rare when I was a kid: a package of food that can sit for *years* and wait for someone to eat it—and when it is finally opened, it tastes the same as when it was sealed shut. As a result, candy, cakes, pies, and doughnuts are rarely more than a few hundred yards away from us, thanks to convenience stores and vending machines. But there's another chemi-cal, invented in 1969, that has since swamped the way we eat and, especially, the way we drink. It contains no vitamins, or minerals, or nourishment—only calories. It's making our lives almost unbearably sweet.

8

MAKING SUGAR

My father died in 2016, when I was forty-six and he was ninety-two. I miss him terribly, but even several years later, I find that I remember him very, very well.

"Coke with chow; wow!" is what my dad would say *every single time* he sat down to a glass of Coca-Cola. When in I was a kid during the 1970s, we didn't drink pop on a daily basis, and when we did, it was part of a makeshift supper when my mother was away from home. Coke with chow (wow) typically involved scrambled eggs and was the first dinner that I learned to serve when my mother was busy attending evening classes in nursing school. "Coke with chow; wow!" he would exclaim every time his seven-year-old daughter set a plate of runny eggs before him, and every time his eight-year-old daughter made him a stack of burnt pancakes, and every time his ten-year-old daughter dished out watery pasta and then covered it in canned tomatoes.

"Coke with chow; wow!" was the tagline of an advertisement that ran only briefly in 1956 but will ring through the ages if my family has anything to say about it. My dad must have first heard the phrase thirteen years before I was born, but I heard him repeat it to me for more than forty years afterward. Now I repeat the phrase to my son every time we sit down with our Pepsis at Target Field and wait for the Twins to start warming up. We chat while watching for signs of life in the dugout, and I tell him stories about his grandfather who used to say, "Coke with chow; wow!"—especially about the year when he turned eighty and was so very happy that his grandson—my son—was born.

Once upon a time in America, most jobs required heavy physical labor. American women, in turn, spent considerable time preparing high-carbohydrate foods for their families. Frying and boiling go quickly, but baking and canning take time. Pies, cookies, and cakes require preparation plus a good hour or so in the oven. The straining, stirring, sterilizing, and sealing required for jellies, jams, and preserves can easily eat up a whole morning, if not a couple of days. When women began to work outside the home, the hours available for housework dwindled, and time-consuming activities such as baking got cut first, since they mostly yielded treats, after all. Accordingly, the amount of white sugar purchased per household dropped between 1950 and 1975. Across that same time period, however, the total amount of sugar that the average American ate each day increased.

Some of the reason for this strange trend has to do with the fact that women were serving more desserts than ever across this time period; they were just serving them outside their homes. During the economic boom of the 1950s, more than one million new waitressing jobs were created. America's businessmen were traveling farther for work, and eating away from home became common, as did the concept of the business lunch. By 2005, Americans were getting one-third of their total calories from restaurants.

But the largest source of new sugar in American history first appeared as "convenience foods"—a term invented by General Foods in the 1950s to describe their new line of foods and beverages that were "easy to buy, store, open, prepare, and eat." These ready-to-eat meals and snacks have come to dominate the supermarket aisles, gas station shelves, and vending machine racks of America. As of 2010, *half* of the money that Americans spend on food goes to convenience foods.

Convenience foods are loaded with sugar. Packaged cakes, cookies, and candies are more or less based on sugar, but sugar is also added to the cheese and sauces that season ready-to-eat meals, as well as to the sausage, bacon, and ham that go into them. At present, three out of four of the food items that Americans purchase have had sugar added to them to make them more attractive to the consumer.

In the 1970s, the average American was ingesting almost one pound of sugar per week in the form of sweeteners added to convenience foods. During the decades that followed, the American workday got longer. As families relied more heavily on convenience foods to meet their needs, the average American's intake of added sugar spiked in 2004 to an all-time high of nearly one and a half pounds per week.

The year 1956—of "Coke with chow; wow!"—seems very far away now. It is difficult to imagine a time when a person's reaction to seeing a can of Coca-Cola sounded anything like "Wow!" By 1993, Coke's slogan was almost a command: "Always Coca-Cola," and for many American refrigerators, this was more or less the case.

As recently as 2007, the average American was consuming one can of Pepsi or Coca-Cola every forty-three hours, and though consumption has decreased since then, every American man, woman, and child still drinks upward of one liter of cola per week, on average.

In fact, most of the rapid increase in sugar consumption between 1962 and 2000 came not in the form of food but as beverages: sodas, sports drinks, fruit punch, and lemonade—Americans increased their average intake of one can of sugary beverage every other day in 1977 to drinking one can every seventeen hours by 2000. Today, sugared beverages are the cheapest (and emptiest) calories that can be purchased and make up a full 10 percent of all the calories that Americans consume.

But why did sugar-sweetened beverages, which had already been on supermarket shelves for almost a century, take off so sharply during the last fifty years? The answer might surprise you: it all goes back to a couple of years of bad weather.

In 1972, a horrible drought parched the vast farm fields in the breadbasket region of what is now Russia. Normal rainfall did not return for years, and sugar from sugar-beet harvests suffered tremendously. To offset shortages, the USSR sought to import both grain and sugar from the outside world and entered the global marketplace for the first time in decades.

On the heels of the drought in Russia, Hurricane Carmen blazed through the tropics on the other side of the world. She pummeled her way across the Caribbean Sea and into the Gulf of Mexico, devastating the sugarcane fields of Puerto Rico and Louisiana. During the years that followed, low global supply of sugar met with high global demand for sugar, and Americans witnessed a huge spike in table sugar prices. Behind the scenes of all this chaos, cornstarch exports quietly doubled in value.

After corn kernels are pulled from the cob, they can be refined into their basic components: oil, protein, and starch. Cornstarch is a chemical with a very simple structure, hundreds of repeating molecules, all in a line, like a string of paper angels for a Christmas tree. In the 1960s, Japanese food scientists perfected a method to slice cornstarch into its individual units, and a second method to twist glucose molecules into fructose. The end product was a syrupy sugar, not a grainy one. It was also a syrup containing extra fructose relative to table sugar. They named this product "high-fructose corn syrup," more simply known as HFCS.

Flustered by the 1974 sugar shortage, America turned to producing HFCS from corn, a crop it had always grown in great abundance. It didn't take many years for America to become the world's largest producer of HFCS; by 1982, the United States was exporting more than a thousand tons per year. HFCS began to take the place of table sugar consumption, and today, one out of every three calories from sugar in the American diet comes from HFCS.

The truth is that HFCS is superior to table sugar for many purposes. Most important, HFCS is a ready-to-dissolve liquid, making it an ideal sweetener for making beverages. As the benefits of HFCS caught on, the amount of American corn set aside each year for milling into starch increased dramatically. In 2001, Americans were manufacturing more than nine million tons of HFCS per year from cornstarch and consuming 95 percent of it as convenience foods and sweetened beverages.

It is not clear that HFCS is worse for your diet than table sugar, but it is clear that table sugar and HFCS are both worse for you than eating nothing. There is no downside, and no risk, to eliminating sugar-sweetened beverages in favor of plain water—and some studies have shown great benefits. And the public has responded. Carbonated beverage sales in the United States were down 12 percent in 2012 from what they had been in 2007, and total sugar consumption has decreased as well. Sugar is faltering in America compared to twenty years ago, but today's figure is still easily twice as high as it was when I was a child during the 1970s.

But let's get back to table sugar, or plain old sucrose, because we are still eating an awful lot of that as well. Fifty years ago, the entire human population consumed about sixty million tons of table sugar. Since then, global consumption has nearly tripled. This year, the United States will import enough table sugar to fill Yankee Stadium three times over. Then what? What happens to all this sugar—and the meat, and vegetables, and grain, and eggs and cheese that we put on our plates? Where does it end up?

Forty percent of it, at least, goes straight into the garbage.

9

THROWING IT ALL AWAY

Pig's Eye, Minnesota (zip code 55102), is not as glamorous as it sounds. Every winter, there's a ninety-day stretch when it doesn't get above freezing outside, and there's usually a week or so when it gets down to forty below. Pig's Eye was founded in 1840 and named after Pierre "Pig's Eye" Parrant, a bootlegger who traded home-made wine out of a caved-in embankment on the Mississippi River. One year later, a French Canadian priest attempted to rename the settlement Saint Paul and officially started the first of many efforts to make Pig's Eye sound like a place where you'd want to live even if you didn't have to. I admit that "Saint Paul" has a nice ring to it, although the story of the city's sewer system is not a very pretty one.

About 10 percent (by mass) of the food that enters your mouth leaves your other end as solid waste. It has been thoroughly transformed during its journey, of course, and contains a large number of bacteria that did you a big favor by helping you to break down what you ate. Your body needs a lot of these bacteria in your gut, but you'll get very sick if even a small number of them get near your mouth. The average adult produces about two pounds of feces and four gallons of urine each week, and all of it must be transported far away and made clean more or less immediately.

The three hundred thousand inhabitants of Saint Paul, Minnesota, produce about thirty-six tons of feces and 150,000 gallons of urine each day. That's enough poo to fill ten concrete mixers to the brim and enough pee to fill one hundred additional concrete mixers flowing into the sewers of Saint Paul *every single day.* The daily slurry of poo and pee produced by the residents of Saint Paul amounts to just one-tenth of 1 percent of the total amount of human excrement produced each day in the United States. All this filth enters the sewers of America, which uses a network of pipes and pumping stations to carry it to various treatment plants, where it is allowed to stew within massive basins. The liquid is pumped into a separate tank from the settled and floating solids, and then subjected to a combination of chemicals and filters until they are clean enough to be released into the bay, or river, or marsh, or whatever the environment might be; sometimes the solids are dried, transported, and then burned. Our Story of More is also a Story of More Sewage. On average, Americans eat 15 percent more food each day than they did forty years ago, which translates into 15 percent more . . . well, you get my drift.

Our analysis of rotting waste can be expanded to include refuse far beyond human excrement. In addition to their massive output of human waste, the homes, schools, businesses, and hospitals of the United States, all taken together, generate about eighty million tons of organic waste each year in the form of discarded fruits and vegetables, other food scraps, and garden clippings. The total for all of the OECD countries is about 150 million tons per year, and the total for all the other people on Earth, combined, is close to four hundred million tons per year.

This means that America, which makes up 4 percent of the world's population, generates 15 percent of the world's organic waste. The OECD countries (European Union, United Kingdom, North America, Japan, Israel, New Zealand, and Australia), all taken together, constitute just over 15 percent of the world's population but generate 30 percent of the world's organic waste. We will see this again when we talk about energy: a minor part of the earth's population has done and is doing the majority of its damage.

There are many points between the farm and the fork where food is wasted. Vegetables are rejected for being too big or too small, grain spills from conveyor belts, milk goes bad on the truck, fruit rots on display, meat expires in the package, and uneaten dinner buffets are scraped into the trash. The more we eat, the more we waste: in 1970, each American wasted one-third pound of food each day, on average. Today, that figure is two-thirds pound. Twenty percent of what American families send to the landfill each day is, or recently was, perfectly edible food.

The business consultants who analyze the efficiency of American supermarkets reckon that one out of every seven truckloads of fresh food delivered gets thrown away. The trucks pull into the loading dock, the crates come out, their contents are unpacked, the shelves are stocked and later destocked into the garbage can, then taken to the dumpster—often by the same set of employees who then turn around and begin unpacking another truck that just rolled in.

The magnitude of our global waste is in many ways equal to our need. The amount of total grain wasted is close to the annual food supply of grain available in India. The amount of fruits and vegetables wasted each year exceeds the annual food supply of fruits and vegetables for the entire continent of Africa. We live in an age when we can order a pair of tennis shoes from a warehouse on the other side of the planet and have them shipped to a single address in less than twenty-four hours; a global food redistribution must be possible.

The problem of garbage shows itself in the numbers— the megatons of food that fester and rot—but there's more to it than that. There is great tragedy in our waste. Every day, almost one billion people go hungry, while a different billion people intentionally discard enough food to feed them. We gamble our forests, fresh water, and fuel on food that we have no intention of eating, and we lose every single time. We annihilate, pointlessly, a countless number of plants and animals that spent the entirety of their short time on this planet in service to our appetites. And in the end, it's also about us.

That half-eaten meal in the garbage—why did we plow that field? Why did we plant those seeds, and water them, and fertilize the soil, and thwart the weeds? Why did we drive the harvester, run the thresher, fill the silo? Why did we deliver the calf from the cow? Herd it to the feedlot? Carry it in pieces from the conveyor belt? Why do we fix the refrigerators, and design the labels, and calculate the vitamin C content, and pave the roads, and change the carburetors so that we can drive, drive, drive meat, bread, fruit, sugar in boxes, bottles, and packages to the stores, schools, restaurants, and hospitals? Why do we walk the aisles, examine, select, buy, slice, mash, season, and serve? We spend our lives on these labors—we wake in the morning and leave our homes and we work, work, work, to keep the great global chain of procurement in place. Then we throw 40 percent of everything we just accomplished into the garbage.

We can never get those hours back. Children grow up, our bodies wax and wane, and death comes to claim some of those we love. All the while, we spend our days making things for the purpose of discarding them. When we cast food into the landfill, we are losing more than calories: we are throwing away one another's lives. It is the ultimate demonstration of how our relentless pursuit of *more* has landed us, empty and exhausted, squarely in the middle of less.

Let's assume, for a moment, that we have a choice. Now let's ask ourselves: Is this how we want to live?

PART THREE

ENERGY

Come, my friend, own how boonless was
the boon; say where is any aid?

—AESCHYLUS (C. 480 BCE)

10

KEEPING THE LIGHTS ON

I have just one thing in my possession that belonged to my grandmother: the 1929 Singer treadle sewing machine that she used every day for decades, to sew pinafores and pillowcases, quilts and choir robes, blouses and bedclothes, to let down hem after hem after hem. My mother bought an electric sewing machine in the 1950s—a Singer 216G. With the benefit of electricity, she taught me the things that my grandmother had taught her. She taught me how to imagine a dress that isn't in the store. How to size myself and map the inches onto newspaper, to extend the pieces for darts and pleats. To measure twice, cut once, pin carefully, then sew. To use the blind stitcher and the buttonholer and to sew with the presser bar raised when you have no other choice. To keep your fingers away from the needle and your hair away from the wheel. To take the tag from an old dress and hand sew it at the back of the neck when you're done, so nobody knows it wasn't store-bought.

It was my mother who first taught me how to transform a dream into a real thing that functions in the world. She learned this from her own mother, on the 1929 Singer sewing machine that is rusting in the corner of my living room.

In my classroom, I like to talk about boiling water because it's something familiar, and the best lessons always start from shared experience. "Suppose you want a cup of tea," I posit. "How many different ways are there to heat the water?" I make a list on the board as I call on each raised hand. An electric kettle, a gas stove, and a microwave are suggested right away, but I ask for still more. A driftwood campfire, offers somebody, and then someone else mentions a coal-fed barbecue. When I taught in Hawaii, students often speculated that there should be some way to usefully boil water by exposing it to hot lava; others knew that you can focus a sunbeam to start a fire and asked whether the heat could be used to warm something but not burn it.

"Many ways to skin the same cat," I end the lesson, pointing to our list, "many different strategies for obtaining the same result." I close with the moral of the story:

"The requirements for each technique are different—electricity, gas, wood, coal, sun—but the result is the same: energy for boiling water."

We use energy every day, not just for boiling water but for many things: to warm and cool our homes, to light our way at night, and even to play a song on the radio. Today, mechanical motors provide the energy that we routinely supplied from our bodies just fifty years ago: golf carts have replaced caddies, can openers plug into the wall, leaf blowers push leaves instead of rake them, and a thousand other examples, large and small, fill our kitchens, garages, offices, and factories. My grandmother's sewing machine is an example of a muscle-powered tool that was once used to perform a daily task. It was first replaced by an electric version, like the one my mother and I used. By now, it has been almost completely relocated out of the home and in the factory. As for myself, I have not sewn together a dress in years.

The total amount of energy that people currently use every day is three times greater than when I was a kid in the 1970s, despite the fact that the total number of people on the planet has only doubled. Much of this energy is consumed as electricity, and its usage is rising fast: the total amount of electricity that people use each day has more than quadrupled over the last fifty years.

Americans are the world's heaviest energy users, consuming a full 15 percent of the world's energy production and almost 20 percent of the world's electricity, despite making up only 4 percent of the world's population.

Those of us who were children in the 1970s in America remember being admonished to conserve household energy. On Saturday morning television, *Schoolhouse Rock!* cartoons chided us to "turn that extra light out," and President Jimmy Carter ordered us to turn down the thermostat and put a sweater on, just as he did at the White House. After Ronald Reagan moved in, energy efficiency—not conservation—became the name of the game. During the decades that followed, our machines (particularly cars, as we'll see in chapter 11) were successfully engineered to produce more work from less fuel. Since then, we have offset what could have been a global decrease in energy consumption by increasing the level of energy we use within almost every sphere of our daily lives.

Today, we watch baseball games inside air-conditioned stadiums, we use elevators to go up or down if it is more than one flight of stairs, and even the book on your lap can draw an electrical current. The total effect is that now not only the tools of our labor but the general objects of our landscape consume energy. Our pursuit of convenience, diversion, repose, or whatever has driven us to live this way is yet another type of *more* that has caused great changes during the last half century.

Every semester I assign the same homework to my

class. "Starting tomorrow morning," I instruct them, "please note down each time you use electricity." My students go home and gamely attempt to do so.

They usually compile at least ten entries before their breakfast ends: flipping on the light switch, using a hair dryer, plugging in the toaster and the coffee maker, and so on. But many of them have given up by dinner, overwhelmed trying to document the barrage of tasks that fill their days at school, at work, and on errands. There's plenty of items they miss: the streetlights at which they stop and go, the water heater that warms their shower, and the array of battery-assisted devices, including not just phones and laptops but everything from the clock on the wall to the speedometer on the dashboard.

When class meets again, we divide our lives into four parts: work, school, recreation, and family. We ask ourselves how each of the four parts are heated, cooled, lit, and maintained. I ask them a difficult question: How much of the working, learning, playing, and being together that you do every day could be done in the absence of electricity?

Electricity is a miracle invention: it allows us to light the darkness in order to extend our useful hours after the sun goes down, it sterilizes the tools that our nurses and doctors use in hospitals, it allows us to communicate with loved ones who are far away. Ever since I was born, I have consumed these luxuries and taken them for granted, and I have lived surrounded by people who are doing the same. One sad fact is that the last five decades of these innovations have failed to bring much benefit to a large fraction of the world. If you are reading this, you are already familiar with the portion of the world that uses too much energy, but you probably know less about the large part of the world that uses too little.

Thirty years ago, there were more than one billion people on planet Earth who had no access to electricity. Today, there are still more than one billion people on planet Earth who have no access to electricity. Because the global population has increased by 40 percent over that same time period, the total percentage of people living in poverty has decreased significantly. Nevertheless, the population that suffers from want is still very large; one out of ten people on planet Earth lives in poverty.

The global geography of need is also unaltered across the last fifty years. When you examine the statistics of hunger, sanitation, disease, and poverty, it is the continent of Africa, with its long history of resource extraction and exploitation, that stands out in both the severity of its troubles and the ongoing lack of solutions.

The Sahara, which stretches all across northern Africa, is the largest and hottest desert in the world. It is the barrier that divides the continent of Africa in half. South of the Sahara, there exist forty-eight individual nations, each with its own government and laws. The people of sub-Saharan Africa number one billion in total, which is just over 13 percent of the global population. However, more than 50 percent of the people on planet Earth who live without electricity live within sub-Saharan Africa. The region is also home to one-half of all people who live without clean water and one-third of all people who live without a sanitary sewer system. Behind these depressing numbers is the fact that while the population of sub-Saharan Africa has more than tripled in the last fifty years, the value assigned to the goods and services produced in the region is both very low and not increasing.

Every day, women and men all over the world work for six, eight, ten, or more hours to produce something of value. The monetary value that is assigned to what each person produces, however, is a complex result of supply and demand, history and greed. Sewing thirty pairs of jeans, performing a tricky surgery, and teaching a child to read are three different labors that could each occupy an entire workday, but the three products—a box of clothes, a successful operation, an enlightened child—are assigned very different values in the global marketplace.

At present, the product of all the labor performed each year by all the people on Earth is valued at about eighty trillion dollars. That's up from about twenty trillion dollars in 1969, which is a quadrupling over the last fifty years. Labor performed by the one billion people living in the United States and Europe is valued as about forty trillion dollars—that's half of the world's value. In contrast, the labor of the one billion people living in sub-Saharan Africa is valued at under two trillion dollars. This means that the 13 percent of the world's population who live in sub-Saharan Africa produce 2 percent of the world's value. Half a century ago, when I was born, the labor of sub-Saharan Africa was also valued at just 2 percent of the world's total. So, while the value of work in the US and Europe quadrupled, the value of work in sub-Saharan Africa stayed the same.

A different kind of trouble exists in India, home to yet another one billion people. Since I was born in 1969, the total value of the goods and services produced each year in India has exploded: it has increased by more than 1,000 percent, while the population of India has only doubled. Despite this explosion in market value, the amount of poverty has changed very little in India. There are hundreds of millions of Indian citizens who have yet to receive any benefit from the global wealth that is pouring into India.

India and sub-Saharan Africa are similar, in that both regions consume very little of the world's energy. Together, they make up 33 percent of the world's population but consume less than 10 percent of the world's electricity. The vast majority of the world's people with no access to electricity live in India and sub-Saharan

Africa. If you had to light a fire every time you needed to cook or clean, and there was no lamp to switch on after the sun went down, how would you go to school or study? It is perhaps not surprising that most adult women who never learned to read also live in India and sub-Saharan Africa.

The rich nations of the OECD sprawl from one side of the globe to the other, occupy almost half of its habitable land area, and are filled with people living well. The sum total of goods and services produced each year by the 15 percent of the world that lives in the OECD is now valued to be worth double that of everything produced in the entire rest of the world. While producing this product, and while living in general, this 15 percent also manages to consume about 40 percent of the world's fuel and almost 50 percent of all the electricity that is generated worldwide.

This imbalance in energy consumption leads to a simple sort of algebra: if all the fuel and electricity in use today were redistributed equally to each of the seven-plus billion people on planet Earth, then each person's energy use could be equal to the average amount consumed by people living in Switzerland during the 1960s. What we saw in chapter 6 with food, we now see with energy: all of the want and suffering in the world—*all* of it—arises not from the earth's inability to produce but from our inability to share.

What was only a faint drumbeat as I began to re-search this book now rings in my head like a mantra: *Use Less and Share More*. As we'll see in chapter 13, there is no magical technology coming to save us from ourselves. Curbing consumption will be the ultimate trial of the twenty-first century. Using less and sharing more is the biggest challenge our generation will ever face.

It is a bewilderingly difficult proposition. It is also the only surefire way we can start to get ourselves out of this mess.

11

MOVING AROUND

Sometimes, when I am sitting on the tarmac at Newark Liberty International Airport, strapped into seat 18G and waiting to take off for Minneapolis (which should have happened an hour ago), I think about all the things I could be doing if I could just get out of this plane. If, instead of flying, all of us—all two hundred passengers—escaped from the plane into two hundred separate cars and drove, individually, from New Jersey to Minnesota, we would have, all together, burned 40 percent less fuel than we ended up using for that one plane flight. If instead of using separate cars, we had boarded a single passenger train, the total journey would have required 50 percent less fuel than required for the gas-guzzling airplane that saved each of us fourteen hours of travel time. Of course, the most fuel-efficient option would be for all of us to have stayed home in the first place, but instead, we've been flying more and more. In 2019, Americans took over two million more flights per year than they did in 2003—and the majority of those flights were for business. With the COVID-19 pandemic came grave concerns about international travel, and during the first months of 2020, international air traffic plummeted to a mere seven per cent of 2019 levels. Within a year, however, airplanes were taking off again and (as of this writing) total miles flown each day is back up to more than half the pre-pandemic figure.

Flying on an airplane has to be the most resource-intensive way you can spend your day, outside of being launched from Earth's surface in a spacecraft. The average American car gets about thirty miles to the gallon; the average airplane gets something like four hundred feet to the gallon. The average plane goes five to ten times faster than many modes of travel, however: cars and trains max out at about eighty miles per hour in most countries of the world. This has made the airplane the world's first choice for long journeys.

Routinely traveling very long distances has somehow become an ordinary thing, even though it was unimaginable to our grandparents. In 1970, the world's airlines carried just over three hundred million people each year, and almost 90 percent of these flights departed from, or landed in, OECD countries. Today, the world's airlines carry almost four billion passengers away from home and back again. More than ten times the number of people will be long-hauled by airplane this year than in 1970 so they can work or play against a change of scenery, at least for a little while.

High-speed rail—that is, passenger trains that exceed speeds of 120 miles per hour—is the only industry able to compete with the airlines for long-distance travel, but consumers tend to choose flying when the extra time necessary for land travel exceeds thirty minutes. On top of that, the United States has witnessed a conspicuous divestment in its railroads during the last two decades: it is one of the few countries in which the total amount of track has actually decreased.

Then, of course, there are cars. If I have a single bias that I should reveal as the author of this book, it is that I hate cars. I hate all cars, and I also hate specific cars. I hate them because they hate me. I don't trust cars, and I never will. I'm also a lousy driver. Which is obviously the cars' fault too. I personally hate cars because all my life, I have watched helplessly as they torture the people I love—I grew up surrounded by broken, busted, and unreliable cars and then when adulthood struck, they came for me.

There are other, and more rational, reasons to dislike cars, however, and foremost among them is the fact that they are outrageously dangerous. If cars were not useful, they would be regarded as a great social problem: more people die from road traffic injuries each year, the world over, than from murder and suicide combined. We condemn and try to eliminate or at least minimize both murder and suicide, but we manufacture and distribute the automobiles that are prone to slaughtering us while we operate them.

Because I hate cars so much, it does not make me happy to tell you that the world currently contains close to one billion passenger vehicles. America remains by far the most car-intensive culture on Earth. In America, six million new cars are purchased every year; in 2017, the car population increased 50 percent more than the American population. When you visit New York City, it may seem as if all humanity is riding the subway, but really only 5 percent of Americans use any kind of public transportation on a daily basis. The rest drive almost everywhere they go.

We drive and drive and drive in circles, some of us all day every day. Where are we going? Mostly, we go to work and back. Eighty-five percent of American adults drive to their workplace, and three-quarters of those who drive, drive alone. Americans have also begun to work longer days and to drive even farther to get there. The average US employee works twenty-one hours more each year than she or he did just a decade ago. We also vacation and visit and sightsee, but most of what our cars do is take us away from the people we love so we can do the things that we have to do in order to buy more gas to put into our cars.

The total distance that Americans drive each year is staggering: in 2015, it was equivalent to five hundred round trips from planet Earth to the (former) planet Pluto. Every day and on average, each American spends one hour in a car. Distance-wise, every woman, man, and child in America will circle the globe by car at least once during the next three years. We spend a good part of our lives in our cars—up until they maim or kill us, that is.

Let's pretend I've convinced you that cars are a murderous joy-sucking plague on the human species. Given where you live, could your family give yours up, even if you wanted to? Could you secure the basics—food, education, medical care, a paycheck—on foot, by bicycle, by public transportation? For the majority of America's households, it wouldn't just be impractical—it would be impossible. The ground rules of American society require cars, and those rules are less flexible than we'd like to believe. While pursuing the ever-elusive *more*, we trapped ourselves into metal boxes. Now we spend our mornings and our evenings maneuvering among the other metal boxes, watching each other through the glass.

* * *

Ford introduced its "Model T" in 1908 as the first family car, but automobiles didn't become truly popular until the 1950s. In those days, the amount of gasoline required to fuel the automobile engine was very large. In 1974, the average American passenger car driving fifty-five miles per hour on the highway (the speed limit of the time) burned a whole bathtub's worth of gasoline every day it did so. At that time, almost all of America's imported oil came from the twelve member countries of the Organization of Petroleum Exporting Countries (OPEC), mostly located in the Middle East and North Africa.

When the members of OPEC got together and halted petroleum exports to the United States in 1973, gasoline prices quadrupled virtually overnight for American consumers, and the whole country was shaken into the realization of its dependence on one imported commodity. As a response, America's auto engineers redesigned the passenger car toward minimizing this dependence, and by 1980, the average car engine was 50 percent more efficient and got about twenty miles per gallon, mostly because the cars themselves were, on average, 20 percent lighter than they had been just five years earlier (it takes less fuel to move less metal).

Motor engines were generally improved during the 1970s, and massive benefits emerged from the car industry's search for fuel efficiency. Airplanes were made 40 percent more fuel efficient between 1970 and 1980, and after oil prices fell to their previous levels, airlines expanded to welcome more Americans on board for long-distance travel.

About this time, a fork in the road appeared, illuminating a possible path toward a bright future. Americans could have remained one-car families and continued to shop locally and fly infrequently, and our total energy use would have decreased over the next several decades as engineering further improved the efficiency of our motor vehicles. As we'll see, this was the road not taken.

Today's automobiles average about 230 horsepower—more than ten times the poor old Ford Model T and more than double the average of the 1980s. The average weight of American automobiles rose sharply as families put minivans and SUVs and pickup trucks into daily use. By the year 2000, the highways were filled with vehicles every bit as heavy as the Lincoln Continentals and Ford Gran Torinos of the 1970s, and at twenty-three miles per gallon, average fuel efficiency was actually *lower* than it had been twenty years earlier.

It didn't stop. Americans bought still more cars and kept driving them, and today they travel twice as far by car each year as they did in 1970. As a result, America's twenty-first-century dependence on foreign oil is higher than it has ever been, while its relations with the countries of OPEC are perhaps the worst we've known. The road not taken was also a Story of Enough, but when given the choice, we recommitted ourselves to the Story of More: America offset any oil independence it could have gained from the miracle of fuel efficiency during the 1970s and 1980s by doubling down, making more automobiles, and proceeding to use them harder.

Between 1970 and 2019, Americans have added forty billion miles to the grand total number of miles they put on their cars while traversing the country's streets, roads, highways, and interstates. Of course, 2020 was a strange and terrible year, when the risk of COVID-19 contagion led to many school and workplace shutdowns, forcing many Americans to work and study at home. Nevertheless, early reports show that miles driven per person dropped by only ten percent during the first half of 2020. No one can promise what the future holds, but the reopening of schools and workplaces, as well as our newfound love for home-delivery, is likely to drive transport miles back up to near pre-COVID-19 levels.

But Americans are not the only ones driving. Between 1990 and 2019, the people of China have added almost as much driving as Americans, to the tune of thirty billion miles per year. Outpacing everyone are the people of India, who have added three hundred billion miles behind the wheel per year, to their annual total.

The total increase in driving between 1970 and 2019,

for the above three countries—the United States, India, and China—required a minimum of four hundred billion gallons of fuel: a volume so large that it would take twenty-four gushing Mississippi Rivers one whole hour to fill it.

The slippery black oil that we slosh into engine after engine after engine has its own story. But to tell it correctly, we have to back up, millions of chapters before page one.

12

THE PLANTS WE BURN

Once upon a time, there was a broad and fathomless ocean. Beneath the waves swirled the currents that flushed salt water in magnificent gushes. Deep in the dense, cold darkness, the seafloor waited with perfect patience to embrace the corpse of every living thing above.

This was called the Panthalassa Sea, and I am certain that the creatures swimming in it believed their watery world to be the entire universe, extending forever in every direction. The creatures of the Panthalassa were different from the ones we recognize in our oceans: jawless fish writhed in great schools, their wormy bodies streaming behind them as they searched for places to attach. Innumerable cartilage forms swam, forever in motion, their gill slits pumping as they moved. Spiral-shelled squids jetted back and forth, contracting and squirting their way along. Sea lilies swayed, tethered to the bottom by their roots, their animal petals filter feeding on the small and weak that floated by.

The Panthalassa Sea was enormous—far bigger than our Pacific Ocean—but it did not extend forever. On the other side of the planet lay the Tethys Ocean, a thick, salty soup of green algae and the tiny animals that grazed upon it. Within this green slime, bubble-encased amoebas drifted from meal to meal, and spongy coral sat anchored, waiting for dinner to pass through. Each tiny alga opened itself to the sun and was fertilized by slough from faraway mountains.

Between the Panthalassa and the Tethys stood a vast continent, drained by rivers, pocked by volcanoes, and home to a different sort of life. Near the middle of this continent stood the Forest of Ruhr, which was altogether unlike the forests we know.

The trees of Ruhr stood thirty feet tall, crowned with fern fronds, spilling seeds from their base. Taller still stood tufted starbursts of needles atop hundred-foot trunks. None of these trees were made of wood: each one contained a hollow cavern of pith. Nor were they covered in bark: their rinds were marked by a paisley pattern of scars. Stranger still, no flowers could be found anywhere—not a one—nor the fruit that follows the bloom, nor the pollen that precedes it.

A mossy carpet lined the forest floor of Ruhr, and

within it, great millipedes chawed dead foliage and ex-
pectorated into the soil. Creatures strange and naked,
turtles without shells, mucked their way through the
fallen leaves, while dragonflies as big as seagulls hovered
above in the humid air. Like the sediment at the bottom
of the oceans, the mud beneath this boggy forest quietly
accumulated, accepting and incorporating the dead, year
after year, without judgment or prejudice.

The story above, for all its romance, is not a fairy tale.
The Panthalassa Sea, the Tethys Ocean, and the Forest of Ruhr are all real places that existed between two
hundred million and three hundred million years ago on
planet Earth. There is not a drop of fiction in my descrip-
tions, for ample evidence has been preserved in muse-
ums. There, you can wander through the history of this
long-ago world, examining its stones and bones.

The Forest of Ruhr grew lush for millions of years; it
was one of the earth's first tropical rain forests. Eventually, it was buried under the accumulating sands of time.
Crushed and rotted, the sludge descended into the deep,
where heat and pressure transformed what had once
been leaves and stems into black, blocky coal. All the
while, the entire continent was pushed and pulled until
its heaving journey stranded it far from home, on the
other side of the globe.

Similarly, the Tethys Ocean was folded down into the earth, and over tens of millions of years, the plants and animals that had died were cooked and pressed into a rich black broth that bubbled in seeps between sandy layers, until a thick crude oil was all that remained of the life that had been. The plants and animals of the Panthalassa Sea followed a similar fate, but their oily remains were abused further, until whole molecules cracked under the strain to produce bubbles. The bubbles slid along the rock layers and merged into great pockets of natural gas.

The plant and animal corpses of the Forest of Ruhr, the Tethys Ocean, and the Panthalassa Sea now constitute the coal deposits of Germany, the petroleum crude oil of Saudi Arabia, and the natural gas deposits of North Dakota, respectively. The largest coal reserve in western Europe was once a tropical forest; the crude oil that gushes from the world's most productive oil wells once lined a shallow ocean; the natural gas collected during today's fracking boom once anchored a deep abyssal sea.

A fossil is everything, or it is nothing, or it is something in between. An insect trapped in amber and a dinosaur's footprint—they both count as fossils, remnants from a time gone by. The bulk of life on land and in the ocean is plant life, and it has been for billions of years. Coal, oil, and natural gas are the pressed, cooked, and cracked remains of the plants and animals (but mostly plants) that lived hundreds of millions of years ago. All of them—solid (coal), liquid (oil), and gas (natural gas)—qualify as fossils. Because they are also flammable materials and can be burned as fuel, we know them as "fossil fuels."

Oil is mostly burned in the engines of automobiles, coal is mostly burned to make electricity in power plants, and natural gas is mostly burned in the furnaces that power factories. Burning fossil fuel is not the only way to power an engine and to make electricity and heat, but it is the most common method in use today. Almost 90 percent of the energy used on Earth—to drive, to cook, to light, to warm, to cool, to manufacture—comes from the burning of fossil fuels.

The world's reliance on oil versus coal versus natural gas is split pretty evenly: of all the fossil fuels burned each year, 40 percent is oil, 30 percent is coal, and another 30 percent is natural gas. The reason for this has to do with the way we build things: more than 99.9 percent of motor vehicles were designed to burn refined oil, the majority of the world's power plants were designed to burn coal, and a great part of the equipment in modern factories is powered by natural gas.

As we have seen, the last fifty years is a Story of More—more cars, more driving, more electricity, and more manufacturing; because of this, it should come as no surprise that it is also a Story of More fossil fuel use. During the last five decades, global fossil fuel use has nearly tripled.

Fossil fuels are also known as "nonrenewable" fuels because the amount of time required to transform living tissue into coal, oil, or natural gas is tens of millions of years at a minimum. When we pull oil, coal, and natural gas from the earth and then burn it inside our vehicles, power plants, and factories, it is not being replaced. Because it is easy to see a world with a growing population as a world of growing use of fossil fuels, we often wonder: How much fossil fuel is still out there?

Geology is a centuries-old science, and the last hundred years have been devoted largely to finding, mapping, and drilling the rocks that contain oil, coal, and natural gas. Based on this work, the "proven reserves" (that is, the for-sure deposits) of fossil fuels have been measured by British Petroleum (BP). More fossil fuels could pop up— most of Venezuela's known oil reserves have been discovered since 1980—but for the most part, the BP databases give a pretty good idea of what's in the ground.

The world's total proven oil reserves constitute a fifty-year supply, given today's rate of oil use. Similarly, the total proven reserves of natural gas would also last fifty years if burned at today's rate. The world's proven coal reserves are much larger: they would take about 150 years to burn through at the current rate of use. Of course, all those numbers are much too high if fossil fuel use continues to increase each year, the world over.

It is true that the total amount of known oil and gas

reserves has doubled since 1980, but global fossil fuel consumption doubled right along with it. We may not know exactly when, but at some point, something will have to give: there is no second Panthalassa Sea that four generations of geologists missed when they mapped the plains, mountains, and ocean floor. If we want human society to outlast the finite resource that it is dependent upon, then any movement away from fossil fuels is a step in the right direction, and one that can't happen too soon.

One thing we don't talk about enough is the lack of overlap between where fossil fuels are found and where they are used, though it has made for decades of war and conflict. The geography is simple, mostly thanks to the final location of the Tethys Ocean. Half of the world's oil and gas reserves can be found within the borders of the nations of the Middle East, with Saudi Arabia as the leader of the pack. Yet, fully half of the world's oil and gas is used within the nations of the OECD.

The contrast between those who have and those who must have oil has made for nearly a century of intrigue between the leaders of Saudi Arabia and the United States, with plenty of allies on each side. As we saw in the last chapter, the economic collaboration of Middle Eastern countries that resulted in the halt of oil trading of 1973 was enough to shake up the American automobile industry for a decade or more, not to mention the role that oil has played within America's Gulf Wars.

Nonetheless, humanity's romance with fossil fuels may represent the greatest resource-based love story of all time. And like a long-married couple tottering off on their final journey through sickness and into death, the concept of divorce is almost beyond imagination.

The United States has met more than 90 percent of its energy needs during the last fifty years by burning fossil fuels. It drives me bonkers that the American conversation about oil, gas, and coal is never about how much we use, only about where we can get more. Today, one-third of the total amount of oil America imports still comes from the OPEC nations: exactly the same situation as before the 1973 oil crisis. We are now, and have been for decades, heavily dependent upon the Middle East for our most basic source of fuel.

America has tried everything to find a way out of dependence on foreign oil—well, except one thing: burning less fuel. Proposals to move away from oil in favor of domestic sources of coal and natural gas have met with strong resistance to the pollution that comes with mining and fracking. Nevertheless, the domestic production of natural gas has increased since 2005, while coal production has stayed at a thirty-year low.

Even after taking into account the rocks beneath Texas, America is not an oil-rich nation: the proven oil reserves of the United States amount to less than 3 percent of the global total, which is bad news for any nation so thoroughly dependent upon the automobile. The United States is rich in plenty of other resources, however, and creative efforts to convert them into "fuel" has given rise to what may be the most wacky environmental inventions of the twenty-first century: the conversion of food for people into fuel for automobiles.

Almost anything containing carbohydrate can be turned into alcohol, given the right setup. This includes sugars such as those from grapes or honey, but it also includes starches such as those within potatoes or barley. Very recently—just since 1990 or so—the edible alcohol "ethanol" has been produced on an industrial scale for the purpose of mixing with, and thus increasing, the gasoline supply. At present, ethanol is produced from processing corn in the United States and from processing sugarcane in Brazil.

This means that tens of millions of acres around the world are planted, irrigated, and fertilized, pesticides and herbicides are applied, picked, and processed—all for the purpose of mashing and rotting the harvest into fuel. It's very inefficient from a resource standpoint: fossil fuel–powered tractors drive millions of miles and apply tons of chemicals to make it happen. The one benefit that these "biofuels" give us is that they can be made domestically and could therefore make a country less dependent on foreign oil.

To some extent this is working, at least for Brazil, which is able to support itself while importing only one-tenth the amount of oil imported by the United States. The United States, on the other hand, imports exactly as much oil as it did in the 1990s, before biofuel technologies really took off. Like most energy inventions of the last one hundred years, development of the corn-ethanol biofuel has been used to increase fuel consumption.

Biofuels are considered "renewable" because every year that we renew the world's agriculture, we get the option of taking a portion of the harvest, mutilating it, and then setting it on fire. Biofuels do not, however, present a realistic alternative to oil at today's level of consumption: if the United States gave up fossil fuels cold turkey and relied 100 percent on biofuels, its current annual biofuel production would last about six days. The story is worse for the European Union: they'd last three days. Brazil could go a little longer—about three weeks, by my calculation. But none of these nations produce enough biofuel to do any more than just take the edge off their fossil fuel dependency, though they are sacrificing a large portion of their national agriculture to it.

There's an additional ethical consideration with bio-fuels, in that using them really does amount to torching a massive pile of food inside the engines of many vehicles. It takes more than twenty pounds of sugarcane to make just one pound of biofuel, and the numbers for corn aren't much better. Today, 20 percent of the grain grown on planet Earth is converted to biofuel—that's a huge fraction for a planet that is also home to eight hundred million starving people, though biofuel enthusiasts are quick to point out that the raw material for biofuel production can and sometimes does include both edible and inedible portions of the harvest.

We are addicted to our cars, and our cars are addicted to oil, and there seems to be no way out. This intensifies when you discover that today's cars are also mostly *made* of oil. The bumpers, the doors, the dashboard, the casing for much of the engine, and the tires are all made from petroleum-derived "polymers." But it's not just our cars, it's our whole lives that are stuffed with, and packaged in, the synthetic material that we call "plastic"—which is yet another product derived from oil.

Each day, the United States imports ten million barrels of crude oil that came directly out of an oil well. These ten million barrels, along with another thirteen million barrels produced domestically, must be processed, or "refined," before they become useful. Oil refinement is largely a chemical process called "distillation": when crude oil is subjected to heat under pressure, it splits into its various parts. The heavier waxy fractions settle, while vapors rise and condense into light fractions such as propane or gasoline, and diesel is left in the middle.

One major by-product of any oil refinery is something called "petrochemical feedstock," the raw material from which plastic is made. It's not an exaggeration to say that the invention of twenty or so different types of plastic since 1950—usually recognizable by the "poly-" in their names: polyethylene, polypropylene, polystyrene, polyvinyl chloride, polyester—has revolutionized almost every aspect of how we live.

Before I give a lecture about plastics, I ask my students to take out a backpack or a purse and count the number of plastic things in it. It is the rare student that cannot find at least twenty items, and it's not unusual for careful pupils to count more than fifty, if they look through the contents of their wallet and separate a ballpoint pen into its working parts. The surfaces that surround us, the fabrics that cover us, the objects that we handle, are to a great extent made of plastics that did not exist when I was born in 1969. Over the short half century that has passed since then, most of the items that used to be made from glass, metal, paper, and cotton have been replaced by plastic, rendering them much lighter, more durable, and far cheaper to produce and transport.

The invention and innovation of plastic truly qualifies as one of the manufacturing miracles of the twentieth century. Plastic surfaces and objects are easily cleaned and kept sterile, leading to their usefulness in hospitals and medical facilities. Plastic film inhibits spoilage and so extends the shelf life of meat and vegetables from days into weeks, allowing for the distribution and consumption of fresh food all year long. Replacing heavy metal auto parts with lighter molded plastics is a large part of what made our cars, trucks, and planes more fuel efficient during the 1980s, though we offset that advantage by making even bigger vehicles and traveling more miles inside them.

At present, global production of plastic is more than three hundred million metric tons per year; that's about equal to the combined total weight of all persons on Earth. Today's total plastic production is ten times larger than it was in 1969, which had grown quickly up from zero starting in about 1940. The majority of plastic produced each year is consumed as disposable packaging. On average, a person living within the OECD discards just over his or her body weight in plastic every single year, and despite efforts to recycle, more than 90 percent of it is simply dumped into landfills. Almost 10 percent of the plastic we throw away eventually finds its way out to sea, where it has accumulated into massive floating rafts of trash that perpetually swirl atop the oceanic waves.

Almost all the world's plastic is manufactured from oil, and oil is used to fuel the factories where it is produced. Making plastic accounts for 10 percent of all the fossil fuel burned on planet Earth every single year.

* * *

When we talk about energy, be it fossil fuels or renewables, it is easy to get tangled up between percentages and total amounts, and I've seen both politicians and scientists engage in this technique. It goes like this: My friend Brian quit smoking a few years ago, which was quite a feat because he had been addicted for decades. At age sixteen, he smoked after school with his friends, and a pack of cigarettes would last him about a week. While at community college, he got a part-time job and so upped his habit to about two packs a week. After graduating, he got a full-time job on a construction site, and soon thereafter he was smoking a pack a day.

When I want to minimize the significance of cigarettes in Brian's life, I emphasize that the percentage of his salary he devoted to the purchase of cigarettes decreased dramatically during the twenty years that passed. When I want to maximize the significance of cigarettes in Brian's life, I emphasize that the total number of cigarettes he smoked each week increased by a factor of seven over that twenty-year period. Both these statements are correct, but when they are presented by themselves, they tend to give different impressions of Brian's habit. To fully understand the role that cigarettes played in Brian's life over those formative years, it is best to understand both sets of facts.

The peoples of the earth, far and wide, are "divesting" themselves of fossil fuels and have been since the 1960s. What this actually means is that fifty years ago, the global population met 94 percent of its energy needs using fossil fuels, and ever since then, that percentage has been decreasing; today, it is down to 85 percent. This is true even in the United States and especially in Europe. I have often seen this set of *true* facts presented as evidence that we are moving in the right direction.

It is also true, however, that the total amount of fossil fuels we burn has increased substantially over that same time period. Globally, the total amount of fossil fuels burned each year has more than doubled over the last fifty years, while the total amount burned in both the United States and Europe has increased by one-third. When we focus on the total amount, we get a clear picture of a planet that is burning more and more fossil fuels every year, but when we put the two sets of information together, as a good scientist should, we begin to see the real picture.

We are using more and more energy, but we have begun to find other ways to get it besides fossil fuels. The magnitude of these "other ways" is no more than a layer of icing on top of a bigger and bigger piece of energy cake that we eat each day. What we never seem to do is stop and ask ourselves if we really need dessert. We've put off that question again and again, while the oil refineries pulse and the world burns.

13

THE WHEELS WE TURN

A spinning wheel is a magical thing that moves and stays put at the same time. If you wrap copper wire around an iron stick and attach it to a wheel, you can make electricity by spinning the wheel near a magnet. This transformation of mechanical energy (the spinning wheel) into electrical energy (the current in the wire) has inspired curiosity since it was first discovered two hundred years ago. So far, the twenty-first century has been, if nothing else, a joyful new experiment with the spinning wheel.

My favorite place to go during summer is the Stone Arch Bridge in downtown Minneapolis. It is a huge granite-and-limestone plaza that spans the Mississippi, linking the center of the city to the University of Minnesota. You can walk, bike, or skate across the bridge, hang out on its plaza and take photographs, or simply sit and people-watch as the river goes by. The midpoint of the Stone Arch Bridge is the perfect place to stop and think about life for a while on a sunny July day.

There's another reason why the bridge is wonderful on a hot day: the spray coming off the rushing water keeps you nice and cool. On the upriver side of the bridge gushes the Saint Anthony Falls; you can hear it rumble in the background. So much water, endlessly falling, is just a brief stumble along the Mississippi River's two-thousand-mile journey into the Gulf of Mexico. No matter how long you stand gazing at the Saint Anthony Falls, you won't see everything, for deep underneath the water's surface, in the darkness, turn five huge wheels.

Each of these enormous wheels is generating electricity, using the wire-and-magnet method described above. As the river falls fourteen feet down over the dam, it turns five big wheels called "turbines." Over the course of 2016, the turbines under the Saint Anthony Falls generated almost a hundred gigawatt hours of electricity—enough electricity to power the city of Minneapolis for a week. There are hundreds of similar "hydroelectric" facilities across America, and thousands around the world, and the basic principle is the same in each one: dam a river, let the water fall down over a set of turbines, then harvest the electricity made by the giant turning wheels.

The largest hydroelectric plants turn more than thirty turbines and generate up to two hundred times more electricity than the small Saint Anthony Falls facility in Minneapolis. Hydroelectricity is a powerful source of energy, and it is by far the most widely used alternative to fossil fuels. Even so, hydroelectric power plants generate only 18 percent of the world's electricity.

But water isn't the only thing that can turn a wheel. If you drive south from Minneapolis toward San Antonio, you'll see clusters of white wind turbines that have sprung up like dandelions during the last ten years. Each blade of these gigantic white fans is the size of an airplane wing mounted two hundred feet above the ground. When one of them catches the breeze, the spinning generates electricity, just like a turbine underwater. The electrical current then flows into our homes, buildings, and factories through a grid of above- and belowground cables.

Wind farms contain hundreds of carefully spaced turbines all working together, and produce about twice the amount of electricity produced by the Saint Anthony Falls hydroelectric station. But compare the number of turbines in the two types of facilities—a few underwater versus a few hundred in the wind—and you'll get a sense of the power of water over air. The total wind-powered electricity generated in a year amounts to less than 4 percent of the total electricity that is consumed around the world.

Solar power can turn a wheel in particularly sunny places. For this, a series of mirrors and lenses is arranged to concentrate and focus sunshine so intensely that it boils water into steam. As the steam rises toward the sky, it flows by turbines, turning them to generate electricity. This concentrated solar power, combined with the electricity that can be produced between the glassy layers of solar panels, accounts for less than 1 percent of all the electricity generated each year on planet Earth.

The electricity generated by solar and wind power is considered green, clean, renewable, and environmentally friendly because no by-products are emitted and for as long as the wind continues to blow and the sun continues to shine, the turbines will continue to spin—that is, no resources are noticeably used up. However, there is much more hype about them than they currently merit: wind and solar power, put together, provide less than 5 percent of the electricity used on planet Earth.

There is one more essentially limitless source for the generation of electricity, but it produces a very dangerous by-product. Naturally radioactive metals, such as uranium, decay and emit energy while they do it. Nuclear power plants trigger this decay within specially "enriched" uranium and extra-large amounts of energy are released. The total energy released is used to boil water into superheated steam, which rises past a turbine and generates electricity. Nuclear power plants are designed to control the speed of the reaction, which is important, because a runaway nuclear reaction is not unlike the detonation of a nuclear bomb.

Eventually, the enriched uranium source will decay to the point where it is no longer useful for generating electricity and must be discarded as waste. This is tricky, because while used uranium does not emit enough energy to turn a turbine, it still emits more than enough energy to be a hazard to plants and animals and, of course, humans. The idea of a malfunction, combined with the toxicity of the waste produced, has led people to both fear and shun nuclear power.

When nuclear energy debuted in the 1970s, it was met with great optimism: an average-sized nuclear power plant generates the equivalent of eighty Saint Anthony Falls hydroelectric facilities, more than enough to power a city of half a million people for an entire year. Then a series of disasters, including Three Mile Island in 1979 and Chernobyl in 1986, showed us that nuclear power—like all technologies—can be just as imperfect as the people who made it. For these reasons and more, nuclear power has been on the decline since the early 2000s. The global fraction of electricity generated by nuclear facilities has decreased from its all-time high of 6 percent in 2002, and several European countries have announced plans to decommission the nuclear power plants that remain.

The United States, by comparison, is still heavily invested in nuclear energy. Almost 20 percent of the electricity produced in the United States is generated by the country's one hundred or so nuclear power plants. The amount of electricity used in the United States that comes from nuclear power plants is nearly double the amount that comes from hydro-, wind, and solar power combined. For all the drawbacks associated with nuclear energy, there is one important by-product that it does *not* produce: carbon dioxide. You'll see why that's important in the next chapter, but for now, let's stick with spinning turbines.

Renewable energy is popular—it is often touted as the "fastest-growing" source of energy with statements such as "the total amount of electricity harnessed from wind has more than doubled since 2010" and "the rate of solar power installation has grown by a factor of more than one hundred during the last ten years." Here we see my friend Brian and his cigarettes all over again: true statements that mask the fact that, taken together, wind and solar still provide less than 5 percent of the world's energy diet, and it's terribly hard to see a way to bring this up to even 50 percent. No, the vast majority of the turbines in the world are turned by the burning of fossil fuels.

Power plants burn coal and natural gas in order to boil water into steam that rises past the turbines, making the great wheels spin; alternatively, gases produced by burning fuel simply stream through turbines specially designed to function at great heat. Two-thirds of the world's electricity is made by turning turbines with fossil fuels. In fact, there are only a handful of countries in the world that do *not* generate the majority of their electricity using fossil fuels.

The discovery of electricity forever changed the way human beings relate to the objects around them. Unfortunately, the conversion of mechanical energy (spinning turbines) into electrical energy (electrical current) is very inefficient. You've probably noticed this if you've ever ridden one of those bicycles at the science museum, the ones that are attached to a single light bulb. You have to pedal like crazy to get even a dim flicker started, and the instant you slow down, it goes out.

The best way to compensate for this inefficiency is to start with a very dense energy source. Fossil fuels and enriched uranium store huge amounts of energy, but a summer breeze or a sunbeam? Not nearly as much. A rushing river is somewhere in the middle. At the current rates of electricity consumption, a modest-sized US city of one hundred thousand people—and there are hundreds of such cities in America—would require the full-time operation of one average-sized power plant fueled by coal.

You may have heard commercials talk about the huge—nearly endless—amount of total energy in the sun, or the wind that causes Earth's air to move in great patterns, but in reality, windmills and solar panels capture only a tiny amount. Powering an American city with a population of one hundred thousand people by using renewable energy would be truly impossible. Ten medium-sized hydropower facilities would be needed. Alternatively, one thousand wind turbines could do the job, or one million solar panels—just to keep the lights on for one hundred thousand people. Of course, all of this assumes that the city is located in a sufficiently wet, windy, or sunny area.

Switching over to renewable energy at today's level of electricity consumption is not possible for the United States, although I've heard people talk about it as a goal. At today's rates of electricity consumption and generation, powering America using only hydropower would require fifty functioning Hoover Dams in each one of the fifty states of the Union. Powering America using only wind power would require more than one million wind turbines, or one every mile or so across the whole of the continental United States. As for solar energy, a land area the size of South Carolina would have to be sacrificed to solar panels in order to generate America's annual diet of electricity. Entirely switching over to renewables at their present rate of efficiency is, unfortunately, a pipe dream.

I do believe that renewable energy is part of the *Use Less and Share More* solution and that there is room to meet in the middle of using less electricity while making a larger fraction of it from water, wind, and sun. However, there's an additional issue associated with scaling up renewables that has to do with where the necessary metals are going to come from. At present, a large part of the cadmium, copper, lead, tellurium, zinc, and lithium used in the turbines that create electricity and in the batteries that store it come from just two countries: Chile and Peru. Historically poor countries, Chile and Peru have remained poor, even as the demand for these metals has skyrocketed in keeping with the sales of battery-powered devices such as laptops, cell phones, and video game consoles.

Other sources of metal might be secured from the mines of Australia, or even Kazakhstan, but the United States will not be able to supply what it needs of these metals from its own mines. This is similar to the problem with fossil fuels, in that lithium and cadmium deposits are not evenly spaced throughout the world, and the countries that are becoming dependent upon these metals are not the same countries that can produce them.

Most of the Americans I meet don't realize that their

iPhone runs off of fossil fuel. When you charge your laptop or phone, you pull electrical current out of the wall, and that current was more than likely generated by a coal-burning power plant located on the outskirts of town. Your refrigerator, toaster, and television, and all the electric lights in your house work this same way, and it's most often the case that they all go back to the burning of fossil fuels, as does the electricity that lights your school, hospital, and workplace and also powers the machines within them. This is true as well for an electric car, too. Linked to fossil fuels through set of wires and batteries made of lead, nickel, cadmium, or lithium, an electric vehicle emits its smog on the other side of town, allowing us to imagine it as clean and green.

If nothing else, fossil fuel use has gotten a lot cleaner over the last five decades. Big steps have been taken to scrub much of the lead and sulfur out of the emissions that are produced during the burning of fossil fuels, and air quality has increased in many large cities as a result. However, the biggest pollutant coming from our power plants and vehicles is something that you can't see or smell, and you might not even notice it becoming a problem.

It's a gas called carbon dioxide, and there's more and more of it every year, and it just might wreck everything.

PART FOUR

EARTH

Attachment to matter gives rise to passion against nature.

—THE GOSPEL OF MIRIAM
OF MAGDALA (C. 150 CE)

14

ALTERED AIR

Every person I've asked has offered me a different definition for "the circle of life." A friend told me how her first granddaughter was born on the same day her own grandmother died and that the equal weight of joy and sadness convinced her that life cannot be lost or gained, only lived and loved. A stranger on the A train busted out with the Disney theme when I asked him. As for me, I automatically think of plants when I hear a reference to the circle of life: specifically of how energy goes in when plants grow and how it comes back out when plants burn.

There's really only one thing that all of Earth's life-forms have in common: their insides burn. Every living organism, from the single-celled microbe to the daisy flower to the hundred-ton whale, is capable of burning plant tissues (yes, plants can burn their own tissues!). The human body is very good at burning plants: we harvest energy from the breakdown of sugars, proteins, and fats within the plants that we eat or within the animals that we eat (animals that ate plants, after all). We use this energy to fuel our bodies, to run, walk, talk, think, breathe, and everything else that we do.

Plant cells—and only plant cells—are also capable of doing the reverse. Plants need, first and foremost, two things in order to live: energy and carbon. Plants get energy from the sun in the form of light and they get carbon from the air in the form of a gas called carbon dioxide. When we burn food in our bodies, we use the energy to live and we exhale carbon dioxide from our lungs. Thus, the dance of life is a two-step: energy and carbon dioxide in, energy and carbon dioxide out.

Inside a tummy is not the only place that a plant can burn. When wood burns in a fireplace, the energy that was originally collected from the sun is released as warmth, and carbon dioxide drifts up and out of the chimney. When we burn fossil fuels—that is, long-dead plants—inside our car engines, energy harvested from the sun millions of years ago runs the engine, and carbon dioxide absorbed millions of years ago is released into the air.

During the last half century of mining and then burning fossil fuels, humans have released a huge amount of carbon dioxide into the sky that would have remained buried deep in the earth otherwise. Since 1969, the nations of the globe have burned enough coal to fill a grave the size of Texas and a volume of oil large enough to fill Lake Pontchartrain three times over. While we used the energy to run countless machines, we also dumped more than one trillion tons of leftover carbon dioxide into the air.

Increases in carbon dioxide are easy to measure— there's a weather station in Hawaii that does it every day—and recognizing the increasing trend in the data is as obvious as recognizing your own name written on a chalkboard. Every single scientist I know is freaked out by the steep increase in carbon dioxide of the last fifty years. But we are more freaked out by the fact that our governments are not as freaked out about it as we are.

We have a saying at my job: "Six months in the laboratory can save you an hour in the library."

Because I research plant biology, I am very interested in the amount of carbon dioxide that's in the air right now and how any increase might affect plant life. After all, the plants around us are more than a decoration— they are food, medicine, and wood: three things that human civilization cannot do without. As the burning of fossil fuels increases the amount of carbon available to plants, there is every reason to believe that agriculture, pharmacy, and forestry could be affected.

During 1999, my team and I designed and built four growth chambers—Plexiglas boxes made with materials from RadioShack and Home Depot. These days, we routinely grow hundreds of plants from seed to flower, monitoring them every few minutes for weeks on end. For the first few years, however, getting the chambers to work at all required lots of trial and error. Keeping them cool turned out to be the biggest challenge.

We designed our chambers to be able to hold large amounts of carbon dioxide gas inside them. While the plants grow, we run a stream of carbon dioxide over them. We need the air to move: we don't want our chambers to become foggy terrariums, we want our plants to feel as if they are outside in a farm field. After we raise carbon dioxide to the right level, we turn on the artificial sunshine. Early on, when we fired up the chambers and walked away, we returned to find that the temperature inside the chambers had shot up past ninety degrees Fahrenheit within an hour of turning the chambers on. We were puzzled: this had all happened inside a building kept cool at sixty-five degrees.

I should have anticipated this. Other scientists had seen the same thing as early as 1856, when Eunice Foote described how glass jars that she filled with extra carbon dioxide not only became "much heated" in the sun but were "many times as long in cooling." A few years later, John Tyndall constructed an elegant brass device that could be filled with carbon dioxide and then subjected to heat; in the end he came up with the same result as Eunice Foote, except he was the one who got the credit for it.

The carbon dioxide molecule has a unique shape that intercepts heat and then holds it. Add just a little carbon dioxide to a chamber of air, then let the sun shine through it, and the whole thing will heat up. This simple fact has been in our chemistry textbooks for more than one hundred years, but it still took me six months to understand it when I saw it with my own eyes.

Scientists have been trying to get politicians to act on this fact for more than one hundred years. As early as 1896, Svante Arrhenius warned that fossil fuel burning would cause global warming. Between then and now, the carbon dioxide content of our atmosphere increased by more than one-third. So the earth should have gotten warmer, right?

It did and it didn't. But mostly it did.

15

WARMING WEATHER

Whenever I think of weather, I think of wind. I think of the balmy breath that wafts down the Mānoa Valley on Hawaii, of the searing gusts that hit your face like a hair dryer in the Nevada desert, of the bracing breeze that washes over the Oslo Fjord, and the chilling blast that greets you just past the Minneapolis airport's sliding doors. I think especially about wind that carries water, about the way the North Dakota sky explodes during a summer thunderstorm, of the horizontal gales of Puerto Rico, of the dumping snow that buries Anchorage in a matter of hours, of the sizzling glare that pulls the moisture from your picnic plate in Arizona, of the chilly mist that makes your joints ache when you so much as look out the window in New Zealand.

Wind is, of course, moving air. Whenever air moves,

it is because something is pushing it or because some-thing is pulling it. You've heard the weather report men-tion high or low pressure systems when there's a storm brewing—that's because air moves from an area of high pressure to an area of lower pressure, creating the winds that move the storm. The energy that fuels the move-ment of wind ultimately comes from the same place where most energy comes from: the sun.

What would it take to make a planet with no wind and no weather? First and foremost, we'd need to turn off the sun. Because the sun shines more directly on the equator than on the poles, and because of the differences in how the sun warms water versus rock versus snow, the temperature of the earth's surface varies from place to place. The sun warms our atmosphere from above, while the surface warms it from below, creating pockets of cold air in the middle that sink and displace the warm air that rises. Every moving parcel of air pushes some other parcel out of the way, so the beating of a single but-terfly wing on one side of the world adds to the breeze that sways through the treetops a thousand miles away. Sunshine also helps pull water vapor up from the ocean into the sky, where it comes back together and falls as rain and snow. For all of these reasons, getting rid of the sun would be the first step in getting rid of weather.

Once the sun was turned off, we'd also need to stop the earth's rotation, as the constant turning of the globe tweaks the winds such that they draw moisture up from the Sahara and rain it back down on the Brazilian rain forest. As a final step, we must also wait several billion years for the earth to cool from the inside out and lose every last bit of the heat from its molten babyhood and radioactive core, for these are what drive the ancient cough of the volcanoes. Until that far-off dawnless day, after our favorite star has fully flickered out and the planet wakes cold and still and dark, there will be both wind and weather.

Because the sun is the primary source of the energy that drives weather, and because of the carbon dioxide molecule's well-understood ability to absorb sunlight, the sensible notion that Earth will get warmer as carbon dioxide levels rise has been dubbed "the greenhouse effect," calling to mind the feeling of being in an artificially warm place.

It may shock you to hear it from me, but I appreciate how the idea of a greenhouse effect—or at least a thoroughly sinister one—can be a hard swallow. Those of us who grew up *cold*—who shivered at the bus stop after closing time, who pushed the old Ford out of the ditch while wearing pantyhose, who walked the back forty for hours, looking to see where the horse got out, and who did all of these things in a thirty-below windchill—are going to be very hard to convince that one-point-five degrees of warming is a categorically bad thing.

I am so often accused of exaggerating the cold climate of my childhood that I recently looked up the National Weather Service records for 1975, the year I started grade school. That was the year a four-day blizzard commenced on January 9 and has since become known as the record-breaking "Storm of the Century." During that terrible storm, a full year's worth of snow came down in one week. In fact, 1977 to 1979—the formative years of my skating, sledding, and snowman-building career— was a three-year span of the absolute coldest winter temperatures ever recorded in the US during the twentieth century.

Minnesota, along with the rest of the Midwest, has become downright balmy since I was a kid, and more and more of what used to be snow now comes down as rain. The season when there's snow on the ground is two full weeks shorter than it was in 1972; the ice covering Lake Superior thaws three weeks earlier than it did in 1905. For a whole bunch of reasons, including too-thin ice, kids don't skate on the ponds in my hometown anymore, but they do sneeze out ragweed pollen for an additional fifteen days more than when I was a kid. There's nothing like visiting your favorite childhood places to sharpen your perception of how passing time has changed the world.

In addition, the effects of rising carbon dioxide are not as simple as the "greenhouse" label suggests. As carbon dioxide absorbs heat, hot pockets of air get hotter. This causes the contrast between warm and cold pockets to get bigger and causes faster evaporation from the ocean, which puts more moisture into the air that eventually has to fall back out somewhere. Because of this, scientists have been predicting an increase in the frequency and intensity of big storms since the 1980s due to increased carbon dioxide in the air. Their idea of "global weirding" makes sense: there are plenty of reasons to suspect that the massive hurricanes, the punishing snowstorms, the drenching downpours, the crazy reverse freezes, and the ruthless droughts of the last two decades were exacerbated by the extra energy trapped in our atmosphere colliding with normal weather systems and then whipping them into a frenzy.

Still, two centuries of burning fossil fuel, and emitting carbon dioxide into the atmosphere, where it absorbs more of the sun's energy, should have raised the overall temperature, right? Yes, it should have, and yes, it did. The average global surface temperature has increased more than one and a half degrees Fahrenheit during the last one hundred years (that's a little short of one degree warming Celsius).

I cannot overemphasize how clear this data is. The instrument used to measure temperature rise—the thermometer—is foolproof: it was invented three hundred years ago and perfected soon after. Weather stations that record the temperature are everywhere, even in the most remote localities of the world, and the data has been faithfully recorded in detail for centuries by devoted farmers, postmasters, nuns, citizens, and scientists. The most recent warming trend of just over one degree Fahrenheit during the last thirty years is not something that scientists disagree about—and trust me: scientists disagree about almost everything else.

The ten-year period between 2005 and 2016 was the warmest decade on record since the invention of the thermometer, placing us clearly at the warmest high of a one-hundred-year-long temperature increase. So far, it doesn't look like 2016 to 2025 will be any cooler. *Somebody should do something,* you might be saying to yourself right about now.

For more than twenty years, the United Nations has been trying to address climate change, and the nations of the world have participated willingly. The first such UN Convention on Climate Change (UNFCCC) took place in 1995 and involved more than 150 countries, including all the big players: United States, China, Brazil, India, Russia, and Saudi Arabia. They had at their disposal the 1992 report of the Intergovernmental Panel on Climate Change (IPCC), a now famous document that described six climate change "scenarios"—six different scientific projections for the year 2100 that ranged from under two to over four degrees Celsius of global warming (that's three to eight degrees Fahrenheit). The purpose of the UNFCCC was to propose widespread changes in energy use and to get the countries of the world to agree to them, ideally under some kind of binding contract.

Three years later, the UNFCCC produced the Kyoto Protocol, an agreement between countries to reduce carbon dioxide emissions back to below 1990 levels. The United States signed the protocol but never ratified it, and Canada withdrew once it became clear that the decrease was not happening. Both the European Union and Russia signed the agreement and then allowed their carbon dioxide emissions to rise regardless. Emissions also increased in China, India, Indonesia, Brazil, Japan, and several other countries that signed but never specified a target for reduction. It was a very nice idea that everyone basically agreed to and then completely blew off.

Seventeen years and four additional reports later, the 2015 UNFCCC produced the Paris Agreement, a climate accord that pleaded for help in limiting net global warming to two degrees Celsius by whatever means available. Every country signing the Paris Agreement was free to chart its own course toward emissions reduction, be it movement toward green technology, reforestation, or simple conservation with respect to fossil fuels. In the end, it was the same old story as before: 175 countries signed, carbon dioxide emissions continued to increase, and 2016 was the hottest year on record.

The problem is that there's no way to enforce an aspiration posing as a contract; so far, nations have gone to war to get fossil fuels, not to keep them in the ground. There's also no short-term economic incentive for using less energy. Fiscal cycles turn much faster than biogeochemical cycles, and there is no industrial profit to be made in pushing a Story of Less.

You may have heard calls to keep the average global temperature rise "well below 2 degrees Celsius"—a phrase taken verbatim from the Paris Agreement. Scientists have predicted all kinds of calamity at two degrees Celsius warming—including catastrophic heat waves, droughts, sea-level rise, ocean acidification and crop failures, and a lot of other things—predictions that could be both right and wrong at the same time. Nonetheless, the idea of such devastation is frightening, and it seems that every new study serves to make the picture worse.

One puzzling response has been to suggest that the answer to our fear is to become *more* afraid and that our real problem is that we're not terrified enough. "People Need to Be Scared About Climate Change" and "Time to Panic: . . . And fear may be the only thing that saves us," shriek today's headlines. I'll be honest, the idea of scaring the public for the sake of scaring it scares me. People don't make good decisions out of fear, history seems to have shown, and at least some of the time, people who are afraid are also prone to doing nothing.

We should also remember that the two degrees Celsius limit stems from a question that scientists asked during the 1970s: How much warming could be expected if carbon dioxide doubled? The answer that they came up with was two degrees Celsius. Their result encouraged other scientists to study the effect of two degrees Celsius warming on weather, agriculture, and society, and they concluded that each would suffer greatly. Avoiding this suffering would require putting a stop to the warming before it got to the level they had studied. This is how the two degrees Celsius warming limit made its way into countless international reports and online articles.

It also refers to a *net* limit: a recommendation that the *total* warming since the Industrial Revolution be less than two degrees Celsius. Earlier in this chapter, I told you that the average global surface temperature has increased by just under one degree Celsius since the Industrial Revolution. This means that, as of right now, we've got just over one degree of warming before we encounter the catastrophes first predicted by the scientists of the 1970s.

My own goal is to inform you, not to scare you, because teaching has taught me to know and respect the difference. I've found that fear makes us turn away from an issue, whereas information draws us in. Thinking logically, in light of the above, it is clear that to avoid warming and upheaval beyond what we've already experienced will require a *transformative* approach to energy use rather than the incremental changes called for in the Kyoto Protocol and the Paris Agreement. We need to transform our collective idea of what energy is *for*, and then transform our individual—and eventually collective—practices of how energy is *used*.

As a scientist, I am supposed to have answers, but like everyone else I know, I cannot yet imagine what real transformation looks like. Almost everything I do uses energy. Almost all that energy comes from fossil fuels. I am one of one billion people who live like this.

If the Story of More becomes the Story of Everyone—if everyone on our planet adopted an American lifestyle— global emissions of carbon dioxide would be more than four times what they are today. It is not certain how much of that carbon dioxide would dissolve into the ocean (and how much damage that would do), but as the scientists of the 1970s found, it is very difficult to envision an atmosphere with less than double today's carbon dioxide content by the year 2200. At least two degrees Celsius of net temperature increase will accompany that rise in carbon dioxide, as well as many of the cataclysms they predicted.

It's not time to panic, it's not time to give up—but it is time to get serious.

The year 2200 is not so far off, just under two centuries from now. Two centuries ago was when we began to use the steam engine in earnest, mining and burning the coal that started this whole mess. Two centuries from now, two centuries ago—four centuries from the beginning to the end, perhaps to *our* end.

Fate has placed you and me squarely at the crossroads of environmental history.

The year 2200 will also be during the lifetime of your great-great-grandchildren. This means that we're down to about five generations to figure out how humanity might survive civilization.

There's a lot more to talk about, and most of it is much simpler than the idea of global warming and weirding, but the stakes are just as high. If you want to get a head start, call up a Canadian during February and ask her what happens when the earth warms. The odds are that she won't mention an increase in hurricanes and forest fires or the expansion of drenching rainstorms and baking heat waves. Given the season and the location, Canadians are much more likely to observe (very politely) that when the temperature goes up, all the ice surrounding them starts to melt.

16

MELTING ICE

There was a while there, when I was six years old, that my best friend was a piece of ice. It was a hard, thick chunk of ice about as big as two bricks put together. I named it "Covington."

We kids walked to kindergarten in the seventies, and though my journey wasn't a long one, it fostered my first thrill of independence as I myself chose which cracks to step on and which ones not to. Early in 1976, I took to kicking a piece of loose ice as I walked, sending it ringing out in front of me every few steps—the frozen North's version of kick the can. One day I arrived at the school grounds with reluctance, having found the perfect piece of kicking ice, its form ideal for my purposes. As the bell rang, I stashed the ice in a snowbank near the fire hydrant. It was still there after school, so I dug it out and kicked it back home, where I left it next to our back door and went inside. I got up the next morning and did it all over again, and Covington was born.

The earth's water is unevenly divided into salty versus fresh. If you took all the water on our planet and shrank it down to fit in a bucket, that bucket would contain one gallon, thick with salt, of sloshing ocean. The amount of fresh water, by comparison, would be three spoonfuls. Of those three spoonfuls, two of them would be frozen into ice.

The global temperature rise that we discussed in chapter 15 is melting the world's ice. Scientists are certain of this, because we see it, using satellites at work, we see it in our daily lives at play, and we see it through our binoculars while on vacation.

Nowadays, the days below freezing in Canada don't last the whole season of any respectable-sized Pee Wee League, so boys and girls no longer play pickup games of hockey on neighborhood ponds. For the same reasons, an ice-skating marathon in the Netherlands hasn't been held for twenty years. Around the world, whole generations have grown up without ties to something the previous generations cherished, owing to too-thin and too-brief ice.

Shuttled into climate-controlled facilities, the most

talented of these young athletes dream of the Big Rink. Should some of them make it to the Winter Olympics one day, it is not unlikely that all the sports will have to be played inside: of the twenty-three sites that have hosted the Winter Olympic Games since 1926, almost half can no longer accommodate the skiing, skating, and snowboarding conditions for the games today. This includes the city where I live, Oslo, Norway, which hosted the Olympic bobsled event just outside my north-facing window, in 1952.

Even we amateur skiers are running out of options quickly. Since 1930, Montana, Utah, and California have lost one-fourth of their snowpack to melting. In Colorado it's much worse: some areas have lost more than 80 percent. Perhaps the United States will follow in the footprints of Germany, Finland, and Norway, where indoor ski resorts are being built (at a wildly high energy cost) to preserve some version of snow play for our grandchildren.

The sculptured ice of Glacier National Park in northwestern Montana has been making tourists swoon since the park opened in 1910, but if you want to see it for yourself, take my advice and don't put it off. Take your family with you, for all the glaciers in the park are on track to disappear within our generation. The regal glaciers of ice that rest across the mountains of Switzerland, Alaska, New Zealand, Tanzania, and Norway (just to name a few) are melting at a furious rate. On average, the earth's glaciers have been losing ice since at least the 1970s, and this melting trend has accelerated over the last ten years. The average glacier in the Rocky Mountains has melted by half since I was born, and many others have essentially disappeared. So many glacial landscapes gone forever, so many photographs that can no longer be taken.

When you think of the North Pole, you probably think of polar bears and Santa Claus, and indeed, one of them definitely lives there. What you may not think of, however, is the shell of ice that floats on the Arctic Ocean. Different in nature from ice that builds up on land, the North Pole's sea ice naturally dwindles throughout the sunlit summer and then refreezes, incorporating recent snowfall during the cold, dark winter. For thousands of years, this pattern of losing ice during the warm season and adding ice during the cold season was enough to keep the North Pole on balance. But during the last half century, all that has changed.

The Arctic melting season still begins near the first of June, but the date of refreezing keeps getting pushed back as temperatures rise. In the 1970s, the melting season ended in September; nowadays, it doesn't end until October. That extra month of melting translates into one fewer month of accumulation. The sea ice that covers the Arctic Ocean has thinned dramatically and its edges are breaking up, which is very bad news for polar bears, who need, among other things, somewhere to stand.

Most of the earth's ice is located at the North and South Poles, where the long, dark winters preserve and petrify each year's snowfall into the preexisting hard, cold ice. Thanks to the poles, about 10 percent of the earth's surface appears snowy white from space. Nonetheless, as the earth's overall warming accelerates, our satellites will observe those white patches shrink and eventually disappear.

Ice melts when the temperature adjacent to it exceeds thirty-two degrees Fahrenheit. This was probably the first science experiment you ever performed, when, as an infant, you reached into your mother's water glass, curious about the shiny cubes. She probably scooped out a few and let you hold them in your tiny hand, and you were enchanted, both by the glassy solid and by the water it left behind while melting.

I lost Covington soon after spring arrived in 1976. I don't even remember the day I lost him. Winter stormed off and the world warmed up as usual; all the ice melted, and by May Day, I had a real-live best friend named Jennifer. To be honest, I don't even remember feeling sad about losing Covington. Perhaps I instinctively knew, long before I studied the hydrologic cycle, that he had gone where all melted ice eventually goes: to be enfolded into the wide, welcoming arms of the open ocean.

17

RISING WATERS

If there is something in the world nobler than a good dog, I have not yet encountered it. All breeds have their charms, but I am partial to the Chesapeake Bay Retriever—big, brown, and indestructible. We put Coco, our most recent Chesapeake, to sleep at the end of her very long life. My husband and son and I sat in a little circle in the vet's office one Tuesday morning. I held Coco in my lap and told her what a good dog she was and how much we loved her. When her breathing slowed, then stopped, and I felt her heartbeat falter against my own, I couldn't help thinking that this was not how I had expected her to die.

Chesapeake Bay Retrievers love to swim—they were bred to fetch ducks from the rough waters of the Atlantic Ocean—and Coco was an extreme example. While we lived in Hawaii, I always carried a coconut with me, for Coco often got it into her head to try to retrieve one of the great red buoys that floated offshore. Once she decided to swim out, a mighty splash was required to lure her off her course and back into retrieval mode, and a big rotten coconut always seemed to do the trick.

She was worst at Kailua Beach on the windward side of the island, where she would occasionally stop and stare out past the surf and across the vacant ocean, utterly bewitched. Thirty seconds later, she'd be off, struggling past the seven-foot waves as if her heart would break, riding the swells and swimming urgently toward California. I once swam out in a panic after the coconut didn't work, chasing her with my best front crawl and hoping the undertow wouldn't kill us both before I could grab her head and turn her back to shore. Exhausted and shaken, we staggered back up the beach that day, both of us sputtering seawater, and I admit that I loved her all the more for her breakneck bravado.

Many more years went by and a frayed old coconut, combined with her love for the woman who threw it, was always enough to tempt her back to land. She is gone now, but I still have dreams where I am standing alone on the shore, watching her swim farther and farther out, until she is a tiny speck that disappears over the horizon.

After talking to my colleagues and looking at maps, I've come to believe that Coco was trying to retrieve the

Waverider buoy that bobbed far out from the seaward edge of Kailua Bay, anchored at depth. I couldn't see the yoga-ball-sized metal sphere with my feeble human senses, but I'm convinced that Coco could smell it or hear the waves lap against it and somehow knew it was there. She was right to want this marvelous instrument. Equipped with accelerometer, radar, and a Global Positioning System, the Waverider is a high-tech instrument built to relay precise measurements of heave, pitch, and roll back to shore and provide valuable information for surfers and sailors alike.

Hundreds of similar high-tech sensors polka-dot the oceans of the world, where they patiently track a wide range of ocean properties, including "vertical displacement," which means that they measure the exact distance from where they float down to the center of the earth, many times each day. A great army of satellites also watches the ocean's surface continuously, eager to record the slightest change in sea level. These instruments have greatly improved the sheltered "tide houses" of old, which were basically floating sheds, often sitting at the end of a pier, in which a ruler attached to a strip chart recorded the height of the surrounding water.

More than a century of sea-level measurements show that since 1880, the average height of global sea level has gone up by more than seven inches. More than half of this rise has occurred since I was born in 1969, which means that global sea level has not only risen, the process of rise is accelerating.

Though the thousands of simple instruments floating in the ocean clearly show this long-term global sea-level rise, it has not been the homogenous process that we might have expected it to be. Because both the ocean and the land are dynamic—waves swell and crash, while the land lifts and sinks—sea-level rise has been much higher than average in certain places, such as along the Texas Gulf of the United States, where the ocean has risen more than eight inches just since 1960. Here in Oslo, the land is rising faster than the adjacent ocean; it is still rebounding from the lost weight of melted glaciers, so the net level of Oslo Fjord has actually gone down by four inches since 1960.

About half of the global sea-level rise that has occurred during the last fifty years is due to water added to the ocean from melting glaciers. The other half of the sea-level rise is due to the warming of ocean surface waters. The oceans have absorbed most of the heat trapped by greenhouse warming, and seawater expands as it heats up. The average temperature of the ocean's surface waters has warmed by more than one degree Fahrenheit over the last fifty years; more than three inches of the total global sea-level rise came just from the swelling of a warmer ocean.

The ocean's creatures have been thrown for a loop by

this warming of seawater: off the coast of North America, the average fish has moved forty miles north and forty feet deeper in search of cooler waters. Of course, this has also changed the business of fishing: the average lobster has moved a hundred miles north since 1970, and many lobster boats have had no choice but to follow.

An increase in sea level has consequences for life on land as well, some of them obvious and some not. When sea level rises, land is lost to the ocean: dry land—upon which we might build cities, hotels, homes, factories, or warehouses—disappears underwater. Just since 1996, the East Coast of the United States has lost twenty square miles of land to the open ocean—a loss of valuable beachfront property. Other effects of rising seas take more time to show themselves: the flooding of farmland and groundwater with salt water forever ruins the fertility of the soil and the drinkability of the water.

At present, one-quarter of the earth's population lives fewer than sixty miles from the coastal ocean. Even with the best protection that engineering can provide—a dike system similar to that undertaken in the Netherlands, perhaps—sea-level rise will likely displace thousands of people during the next hundred years and make drinking the local water and farming the adjacent fields impossible for many thousands more. These effects will hit worst in areas where the land is low or sinking and where people are too poor to undertake construction measures.

The river-delta nation of Bangladesh lies just barely above sea level. Within its borders, a population half the size of the United States ekes out a living from a piece of land the size of Alabama. If the sea continues to rise, the area of Bangladesh is likely to shrink by 20 percent over the next thirty years, crowding people into even less land and fewer resources. Incidentally, the people of Bangladesh produced far less than 1 percent of the carbon dioxide emitted to the atmosphere during the last fifty years, yet they are poised to pay the highest price incurred by its effects. This is a common trend: the people benefiting from the use of fossil fuels are not the people who suffer the most from its excess.

Carbon dioxide has not only affected the ocean through warming, it has altered it directly by soaking into seawater. Almost one-third of the carbon dioxide produced from the burning of fossil fuels was absorbed by the ocean, like the way carbon dioxide gas is injected into Coke (with chow; wow!) to make it fizzy. Your dentist has probably warned you that drinking soda is bad for your teeth, and part of the reason is that carbon dioxide reacts with water to form an acid that eats away at your enamel. This same thing is happening in the ocean, as the increased acidity of seawater has destroyed coral reefs around the world, making it harder and harder for shelled marine animals to grow and maintain their hard parts. As we go about our business burning fossil fuels, more carbon dioxide enters the atmosphere, and thus the ocean, every day.

Back to melting for a moment: Remember how half of the sea-level rise that has occurred during the last fifty years is due to water being added from melting ice? The ice that *already has* melted and entered the ocean, causing a rise in sea level that displaced thousands of people, amounts to less than 5 percent of the ice that *could* be melted by future warming.

All the ice that I mentioned in chapter 16 (namely, the world's glaciers and the sea ice covering the Arctic Ocean) is dwarfed by the vast ice fields that blanket Greenland and the continent of Antarctica. The wide expanse of ice that covers the rocky surface of Greenland has begun to falter: like the rest of the Arctic, it is melting, losing billions of tons of ice each year. Fortunately, for now, some of this meltwater refreezes as it runs across the surface of the ice sheet, but some does enter the ocean.

And then there's the Antarctic ice sheet, fields of ice that are more than a mile deep and a million years old, on which stand a full 90 percent of the ice on planet Earth. So far, we have seen less melting in Antarctica compared with the Arctic, but this could change: radar sounding waves have shown that the ice is beginning to peel away from the portion of Antarctica that faces the Pacific Ocean. Should continued warming melt the Antarctic ice sheet in earnest, the amount of water released into the ocean, and the sea-level rise that follows, will be massive.

The global records of carbon dioxide, temperature, ice mass, and sea level are large data sets from simple measurements that show an obvious trend over the last twenty years, and yet somehow, they also give rise to nonstop drama. I can't turn on my computer without hearing about climate deniers and their lack of brains and sophistication. I can't click on any of the links within without hearing even more about climate alarmists and their hypocrisy and hyperbole.

Separated into two camps, we flame each other across the internet as if the atmosphere cared what we think, as if we could shout the rising waters back up into the glaciers they came from, as if winning an argument accomplishes something in and of itself.

In the meantime, scientists continue making the observations and taking the measurements that show what is happening. I won't lie to you—it's a tough job. Today's climate scientist is more like a worried oncologist than like an Indiana Jones or a Jacques Cousteau. The earth is sick and we suspect that it's something bad. This heat, this melting, this flooding, these hurricanes, those blizzards—they are not normal, and we need to do the tests that allow for a firm diagnosis and a treatment plan. We hope that it is not as bad as it looks, but we need some support, cooperation, and a little patience to get to a definitive answer.

The carbon dioxide level of the atmosphere is higher than it has been at any time during the last million years. The ice is melting, the sea is rising, and the weather has begun to falter. Our earth is unwell. Its symptoms are worrying and will not improve on their own. We have all but used up the brief window when we can act, and we are running out of time. I know this because many of the things around us have already started to die.

18

THE BIG GOODBYE

I was fully prepared to encounter plenty of dead fish when I opened the door of the PUCRS Ichthyology Lab in Porto Alegre, Argentina, in 2005. What I wasn't prepared for was the smell. It was enough to make your eyes water. It was impossible to focus on anything but the overpowering smell of booze. That lab smelled like the inside of a vodka bottle—if the bottle had been immersed in a bathtub of whiskey and sunk to the bottom of an ocean of gin.

The Pontifícia Universidade Católica do Rio Grande do Sul (PUCRS) is located in southern Brazil, just near the mouth of the Jacuí River. It contains a state-of-the-art laboratory that has been assigned the task of making an up-to-date list of the freshwater fish of South America. It is one of many institutes created for the sake of documenting the incredible diversity of plants and animals that exists within the borders of Brazil, a land so filled with butterflies, insects, flowers, fish, and amphibians that it has stretched the imagination of modern biologists completely out of shape.

As of today, thousands of species of freshwater tropical fish are known to exist, and about half of them live in Brazil. Of those living in Brazil, the great majority is also *endemic* to Brazil—which means they are native species living in their original habitat, a rare thing in this age. The PUCRS lab that I visited was chin-deep into its collection project: teams of students had set nets across the rivers of southern and eastern Brazil. From each of these rivers they hauled hundreds of fish back to the lab, sorted them into piles, and preserved them in alcohol until they could fully examine and describe them all. The variety of what they brought home in those nets was brain-boggling. For most scientists, identifying a new species is a career-changing, once-in-a-lifetime event; these South American biologists were discovering a new species, on average, once every four days.

Against every wall—of the lab, of the hallway, on the balcony—stood a line of white plastic barrels, tall as my shoulders. A single handle was attached to the top of each lid, and when you lifted it, up came forty or more fishing lines, each one with a dead fish at the end. I would have been only mildly surprised to see a fish floating in the coffee cup that my tour guide was drinking from.

"Will you ever process all of these?" I asked her as she began the paperwork for the latest batch.

"Eventually, yes," she assured me, sipping from her coffee cup. "We already see them tapering off, in fact." She added, by way of explanation, "A lot of what we do here is about looking a fish in the face at least one time before it goes extinct."

There's a reason that the PUCRS lab is trying so hard to count and describe the endemic fish of Brazil: they are the canary species in the ecological coal mine. Freshwater habitats make up less than 1 percent of Earth's surface but contain at least 6 percent of our planet's species. The number of endangered species within freshwater habitats is greater, proportionally, than in the land and ocean combined.

The Jacuí River, which flows past the PUCRS lab and joins with Lake Guaíba on its way to the Atlantic Ocean is a pretty typical Brazilian river located near a populated area. In 2000, the upper waters of the Jacuí were stopped up when the Dona Francisca Dam was built. On the upriver side of the dam, five thousand acres of land were flooded to create the Dona Francisca reservoir, and more than five hundred families had to relocate their homes as a result.

Dams are built for all kinds of reasons, but they all result in the same thing: an upstream lake where there previously was none. Lake water is more accessible than flowing water because it can be used in volume to irrigate crops, water animals, and wash or cool machinery inside factories. Dammed-up lake water can also be released over the dam to generate electricity, as described in chapter 13. Dams are built to support industry and agriculture, and by doing so, they almost always bring on more industry and more agriculture.

When a dam is built, life downriver is forever altered. The most obvious change is that the volume of flowing water is reduced to a fraction of what it was when the river was running freely. Once a river's flow is reduced, the space available to fish, insects, and amphibians is also reduced. Crowding follows, competition for food and space increases, resources become strained, and many of the river's inhabitants die. Hence the race against time within the biology labs of Brazil: they want to figure out which fish are there today, so that we will know which ones have disappeared tomorrow.

Extinctions are part of the natural course of action on planet Earth; a new food source or living space opens up, and this creates an open niche. A subset of one species has the skills for a life in the niche, they move in and breed amongst themselves, and before long, a new species is born. Eventually, the niche closes after the environment changes or a stronger competitor moves in. Once the niche is gone, its dedicated species decline and eventually go extinct. Paleontologists see this process over and over in the rocks containing fossils through the ages: species are constantly popping up and constantly disappearing. The average species persists for something like ten million years before going extinct. Because this cycle of emergence/extinction has been in place for more than three billion years, many more species have been lost to extinction than are in existence today.

Once in a blue moon, a whole bunch of niches will close at the same time, triggering what is known as a "mass extinction." The fossils of the last five hundred million years show evidence for five such catastrophes: mass extinctions during which 70 percent (or more) of existing species were lost to extinction, all at once. Earth's most recent mass extinction occurred about sixty-six million years ago and resulted in the disappearance of the dinosaurs. Based on the rate of decline that we see in the species of today, we fear we are moving toward a sixth mass extinction.

The surveys of the last few decades show a disturbing trend: a decline in more than half of all bird and butterfly species and a decline in one-quarter of all fish and plant species. We are witnessing rapid losses before our very eyes, from the base of the food chain on up. For several species, we have seen wild populations decline clear into extinction: the thicktail chub, the Rocky Mountain locust, the Japanese sea lion, the black softshell turtle, and the stringwood tree, just to name a handful.

The first reason for today's decline in species is the widespread loss of habitat; expanded cities mean fewer places for plants and animals to live. Since the first Europeans showed up, North and South America have lost 88 percent of their tropical forests, 90 percent of their coral reefs, and 95 percent of their tall-grass prairies. The species that were adapted to those niches have all but vanished now. The cities, suburbs, harbors, and farm fields that we built in their place presented brand-new niches, ones just right for the "invasive" microbes, insects, plants, and animals that came in with Europeans during the 1600s and 1700s.

The second reason for modern species decline is the climate changes that we covered in chapter 15. Extreme heat waves have been known to kill whole colonies of bats, and disappearing polar ice has wrecked the hunting ground of polar bears. Increased carbon dioxide fertilize the growth of poison ivy over that of native trees, and the future of green sea turtles has been doomed by the warming that converts their eggs into female spawn (only). In many cases, previously natural areas have been made over into more uniform and boring lands of concrete, asphalt, ditch, yard, and hedge. Within them, just a few non-native "weeds" flourish at the expense of the endemic originals.

One important thing that separates a mass extinction from a more run-of-the-mill extinction is the rapid pace of species loss. In a mass extinction, the total species loss occurs over thousands of years instead of the millions that pass while background extinctions come and go. The current rate of global species extinction is almost one thousand times higher than the background rate that paleontologists count within the rocks of the past. If we project forward from today's rate of loss, by year 2050 we will have lost one-quarter of today's species to extinction; that's one-third the number needed to meet the definition of a mass extinction.

At the end of a mass extinction, the tree of life has lost several branches—and yet, afterward, life does go on. Plants regreen the earth and animals repopulate the oceans; different species take over and different landscapes result; and time resumes its forward march. There will be life on planet Earth after the sixth mass extinction, but we are not able to imagine it any better than the dinosaurs could have imagined a world dominated by mammals walking on two legs, driving bulldozers, and flying airplanes.

All species will go extinct eventually, even our own: it is one of nature's few unbendable rules. As of today, however, the train has not quite left the station. We still have some control over our species' demise—namely, how long it will take and how much our children and grandchildren will suffer. If we want to take action, we should get started while it still matters what we do.

19

ANOTHER PAGE

When I was a little girl, my father told me that one day, all the people on Earth will live together, free from war and hunger and need. When I asked him when it would happen, he said he wasn't sure but that he was sure the day would come.

These many years later, I wonder if he chose that day, in particular, to talk to me. I had just turned nine, which made me old enough to question his views but still young enough to listen to his answers.

"How?" I asked him; I was skeptical. "We all live in different countries," I observed, "and we all speak different languages."

"Borders can change," he responded quietly, "and we can learn each other's languages." He added, "We are a species that can learn anything."

I was his youngest child, his only daughter, and I had come to him late in his life. He was fifty-five years old when we had this conversation and had already seen the world map revised twice during his lifetime. But this was not the only reason he believed in our ability to transform the world.

He believed it because he had seen people grow and change when he taught physics, chemistry, calculus, and geology to an entire generation of our town and then to the entire generation of their children. He believed it because of what he had seen during his own life: the magic of radio had become television, the telegraph became the telephone, the computer with ticker tape became the computer with punch cards, which eventually became the magic of the internet. He believed it because of his family: his children had a mother who had survived their birth (unlike his grandmother), would have the opportunity to go to college (unlike his parents), and were growing up free from the shadow of polio (unlike him).

He believed it because he loved me, and because of him, I believe it too. I believed my first, and my fondest, science teacher when he told me that when we finally devote ourselves to work and to love, even our most fantastic dreams will eventually come true.

* * *

Multiple solutions have been proposed to decrease the amount of carbon dioxide in the atmosphere in the hopes of limiting—and ultimately reversing—the earth's rising temperatures, and all of these solutions show some promise. It is possible to separate carbon dioxide from air, concentrate it, and then seal it in a container; the torpedo-shaped metal tanks standing next to a restaurant's soda dispenser are an example of this—they are full of concentrated carbon dioxide. Engineers have proposed to remove carbon dioxide from the atmosphere and then inject the liquid deep into the earth, where it would remain forever trapped between layers of rock at the bottom of the ocean or in the caverns left behind after drilling for oil and mining for coal. The problem, so far, is that this process of trapping, condensing, transporting, and then injecting takes more energy than it compensates—that is, the amount of fossil fuel that you have to burn within machinery, truck engines, and power drills to make it happen is more than the amount of burned fossil fuel you are able to trap in the end. Nevertheless, several nations continue to refine these "carbon capture and storage" methods into something that might someday break even.

Equally interesting is the notion of drawing down carbon dioxide by enhancing rock weathering: every year, a small amount of carbon dioxide naturally leaves the atmosphere to mix with rainwater. This yields a weak acid that trickles down into the soil and dissolves the bedrock at its base. Scientists have proposed to increase the amount of rock surface area available for weathering by grinding up volcanic minerals and then dusting the debris across the tropical forests and farm fields of India, Brazil, and Southeast Asia. As with carbon capture and storage, however, the energy used in grinding, transporting, and spraying millions of tons of rock dust would outbalance any gains that were made in carbon dioxide reduction, at least for several centuries.

One popular solution is to stimulate plant growth, to naturally pull carbon dioxide out of the atmosphere and transform it into living plant tissues, such as cell walls, and leaves and wood. This is what trees do by growing on land, and it is what algae do by growing in the ocean. Multiple offers are available for people to offset the carbon dioxide produced when they fly, by paying money for trees to be planted. This is an appealing concept—after all, who doesn't like the idea of more forest?—but the numbers don't work out very well. First of all, the rewards are very slow to kick in, as most tree seedlings take decades to grow into a respectable tree with many leaves and much wood. Furthermore, trees don't permanently trap very much carbon dioxide into their tissues, as most of the leaves and needles that fall to the ground each year shrivel up and decay, releasing the carbon right back into the atmosphere as carbon dioxide. The most stable stash of fixed carbon dioxide in the forest is the tiny amount of rotten plant material that makes it into the soil, and new soil takes hundreds to thousands of years to form. Planting trees will offset your energy use, but it won't pay off during your lifetime and possibly not during your children's lifetimes, either.

More promising is the idea of fertilizing plant growth on the ocean's surface: there are vast areas of the Pacific Ocean that lack only one or two key nutrients and could be stimulated to yield huge colonies of green algae and phytoplankton within weeks—tiny plants that would eventually die and sink to the bottom of the ocean, effectively trapping the carbon dioxide that they used to form their tissues. Seeding tropical waters with iron or phosphorus could trigger such blooms, but the exact amount of carbon dioxide that could be trapped is uncertain, as are the consequences for ocean life, including the fish that we depend upon as a food source.

An alternative approach for reducing the earth's temperature is to reduce the amount of incoming sunlight—to simply block the sun's energy before it interacts with Earth's atmosphere. Ideally, this approach would allow for cooling without requiring any changes in fossil fuel use. Many ways of blocking the sun's rays have been proposed, including launching a huge sunshade into orbit to reflect heat outward, similar to the shade you place under your car's windshield on hot days. Another idea is to spray aerosol particles high above the clouds, in much the same way that Mount Pinatubo did in 1991 when it erupted, leaving a layer of haze that cooled portions of the planet by almost one degree Fahrenheit for two full years. These approaches have the advantage of being quick and resulting in substantial cooling almost immediately. They are, however, incredibly risky: tinkering with the heat balance of the atmosphere is almost certain to disrupt weather, and less precipitation and more frequent droughts are the last things we need for global agriculture.

As for dealing with sea-level rise, there is already a long tradition of engineering cities such as Amsterdam to resist flooding, but the techniques are expensive and out of the reach of many poor countries, such as Bangladesh. Novel constructions have been proposed to directly reduce the melting of polar land ice, which will likely be the main source of added ocean water during the next several centuries. These constructions include a concrete wall in western Greenland to prevent warm seawater from coming into contact with the glaciers' base. Even more ambitious is the proposed plan to prop up the icy edges of West Antarctica from underneath via an artificial island anchored to the seafloor. The idea is that such a prop would keep the ice sheet whole and prevent it from breaking into pieces and then melting.

Moving tons of concrete and gravel and using heavy

machinery into polar regions seems outrageously expensive, but perhaps not so much when we consider that the cost of the world's largest construction projects, such as the Hong Kong International Airport or the hydroelectric Three Gorges Dam, which commonly run to twenty billion and thirty billion dollars.

Regarding the crisis in species decline, nothing has been shown to prevent extinctions so well as simply protecting habitats from human access and development. About 13 percent of Earth's land area is currently under some degree of legal protection, which is more than triple the amount that was protected forty years ago. Ecologists believe this has reduced extinction rates in mammals, birds, and amphibians by as much as 20 percent of what they would be otherwise. Multiple nations are also considering the establishment of marine protected areas, conserving swaths of ocean from both fishing and shipping transport.

None of the solutions above, however, address the root of the problem or could alter our future the way a serious shift toward energy conservation could. I mentioned back in chapter 10 that if all the fuel and electricity in use today were redistributed equally across the earth's population, global per capita energy use would be equal to the average consumed in Switzerland during the 1960s. If, instead of waiting for this imaginary redistribution, the countries of North America, Europe, Japan,

Australia, and New Zealand reduced their energy use to that level now, total global energy use would plummet by at least 20 percent, as would carbon dioxide emissions.

The changes to daily life required to meet this reduction would be most keenly felt in the United States, where energy use per capita is the highest in the world. Each American would need to forgo four out of every five plane rides, and travel via mass transportation at least fifty times farther each year than they do now. The United States as a whole would have to get rid of at least 30 percent of its motor vehicles, and the resultant effect on the trucking industry would require that we eat and shop from an entirely different set of goods.

The good news is that there is no reason to think that energy conservation will necessarily reduce our quality of life: life expectancy in Switzerland back in 1965 was similar to that of today's America and much higher than the current global average. Workdays were shorter, as were commuting distances. Life was not perfect then, but the basics of a healthy life were already in place at a much lower level of fossil fuel use.

As a solution, energy conservation by its very definition requires the least effort of any approach. It is a strong lever by which we could pull ourselves back into alignment with a future that our grandchildren might survive. There's only one problem: driving less, eating less, buying less, making less, and doing less will not create new wealth. Consuming less is not a new technology that can be sold or a new product that can be marketed, and acting as if it can be is absurd. Economic proposals such as the "carbon tax" and other attempts to provide money incentives against fossil fuel use have been met with opposition from industrial sectors.

It's no use pretending that conserving resources isn't at direct odds with the industries that helped to write our Story of More and that increasing consumption over the last fifty years wasn't tightly coupled to the pursuit of *more* profit, *more* income, *more* wealth. It's time to look around and ask ourselves if this coupling is truly the only way to build a civilization, because the assumption that it is may represent the greatest threat of all. Each one of us must privately ask ourselves when and where we can consume *less* instead of *more*, for it is unlikely that business and industry will ever ask on our behalf.

None of the solutions discussed here, alone, will be a silver bullet capable of saving us from the dark specter of hunger, want, and suffering that unabated consumption is likely to bring about. All measures of conservation, as well as all technologies meant to distance us from fossil fuels, are worth pursuing, in the same way that doing something is always more than doing nothing. We need everyone, not just scientists, to start thinking about tomorrow. We need to figure out not only the possibilities associated with each solution but also the risks, so that whenever we have the chance to act, we can do so with our eyes open and our understanding as full as we can make it.

Earth—the only thing we all share—has become a pawn in our political discourse, and climate change is now a weapon that can be hurled by either side. For scientists especially, feeding into political polarization damages the planet we are trying to save. Down the road, it won't matter what we do as much as it matters what we *all* do. Need I mention that "we all" has always included—and always will include—both me and you? We are all part of what is happening to the world, regardless of how we feel about it, regardless of whether we personally "believe" or "deny." Even if you consider yourself on the right side of environmental issues and a true believer in climate change, chances are that you are actively degrading the earth as much as, or more than, the people you argue with. An effort tempered by humility will go much further than one armored with righteousness.

During each of the years that I've taught this material, at least one student—overwhelmed by the data—would come to my office and ask me if I thought there was any hope for planet Earth. Here is how I would answer:

Yes. Absolutely. I do believe there is hope for us,

and you are very welcome to take some and keep it for your own.

I am hopeful because my life is filled with people who also care about these issues. The smartest people I know are dedicating their lives to gathering the data that will tell us more. This very day, scores of people got to the lab early and will stay late, trying to quantify the exact magnitude of sea-level rise, warming weather, melting polar ice. They are walking the fields and counting what is there and what is not. The ecologists who first noticed these patterns could not have imagined the computers or instruments that we now use every day. We are watching and working and not just worrying. Climate science is a part of science, after all, and science is now just as it has always been: overworked and underfunded and absolutely unwavering in its refusal to ever stop trying to figure it all out.

I am hopeful because history teaches us that we are not alone. During centuries past, women and men railed helplessly against overwhelming forces that poisoned the wells, spoiled the crops, and robbed them of their loved ones. We may discount their science as superstition, but it was based on state-of-the-art observations and earnest conclusions. Genetically, we are no smarter than they were, and we may be laboring in similar darkness. The succeeding centuries did bring solutions to even the worst of these ancient plagues, and though the solutions came far too late for many, they were not too late for all.

Then comes the hardest part of the conversation, when I ask them to think about their own lives.

I remind them: We are strong and lucky. Our planet is home to many who struggle to survive on too little. The fact that we are of the group with food, shelter, and clean water obligates us not to give up on the world that we have compromised. Knowledge is responsibility.

I ask them: What will you do with the extra decade of life given to you, over and above your parents'? We, the 20 percent of the globe that uses most of its resources, must begin to detox from this consumption, or things will never get better. Look at your own life: Can you identify the most energy-intensive thing you do? Are you willing to change? We will never change our institutions if we cannot change ourselves.

I stress one thing above all else: *Having hope requires courage.* It matters not only what we do about global change but how we talk about it, both in the classroom and beyond. We risk our own paralysis with the message that we have poisoned the earth and so the earth rejects us. As far as we know, this is still our species' eternal home, and we must not alienate each other from it. We must go forward and live within the world that we have made, while understanding that its current state arises from a relentless Story of More. We can make this easier by being kind to one another along the way.

Now is the time to imagine a world in alignment with our ideals, as we settle in to this new century. We will need to feed and shelter ourselves and one another, but everything else is on the table. What can seven billion people do that three billion people could not? is the question of my life so far. We are troubled, we are imperfect, but we are many, and we are doomed only if we believe ourselves to be. Our history books contain so much—extravagance and deprivation, catastrophe and industry, triumph and defeat—but they don't yet include *us*. Out before us stretches a new century, and its story is still unwritten. As every author will tell you, there is nothing more thrilling, or as daunting, as the possibilities that burst from a blank page.

APPENDIX:
THE STORY OF LESS

Our healing is not in the storm or in the whirlwind, it is not in monarchies, or aristocracies, or democracies, but will be revealed by the still small voice that speaks to the conscience and the heart, prompting us to a wider and wiser humanity.

—JAMES RUSSELL LOWELL (1884)

I. THE ACTION YOU TAKE

Now, after all you've read, I have one question for you: Do you want to live in a more equitable world with a brighter future?

If your answer is Yes, then there's a lot you can do to get there, bearing in mind that while Rome wasn't built in a day, it didn't burn down in a day, either.

Step 1: *Examine your values.*
A large number of issues have been raised in these nineteen chapters. Which ones resonate with your daily life, your greatest fears, your highest aspirations? Consider them all, then rank them accordingly. Where does world hunger fall on your list? Extinction of species? Weirding weather? Green energy? Pollution of our oceans? Animal rights? Public transportation? Beach erosion? Healthy school lunches? National parks? Organic farming? Arctic warming? Women's health? Some of these issues may be very important to you and others less compelling. Identify one issue to focus upon: the one that you are willing to sacrifice for.

Step 2: *Gather information.*

Go through your habits and possessions to take stock of how your personal life matches (or like most of us, doesn't match up with) your values. How many miles does your family drive? How often do you fly? Is any of it optional? How much of the water that goes down your drain is still drinkable? How much of the food that goes into your garbage is still edible? How much meat do you eat, and how often? Go through your closet and look at the tags: Where were your clothes made? How far did they travel to get to you? Go through your refrigerator: How many items came to you in a plastic container? How many of them contain added sugar, posing as "natural sweetener," "corn syrup," "cane sugar," "cane syrup," "maltodextrin," "fruit juice concentrate," "raw sugar," "brown sugar," "dextrose," "glucose," "HFCS"? Is there land near you that is being contested for development versus conservation? How is the electricity that comes into your house generated? Is constructing a "renewable energy" facility up for discussion within your county? Where does the gasoline you pump come from? Is any of it ethanol? Which of the meats that you consume concentrates the most grain? Which parts of your sushi were likely raised inside a farm?

Step 3: *Can you make your personal activities consistent with your values?*

Pick out one change that you can make. Can you drive fewer miles? Carpool? Eliminate some of your plane trips? Use public transportation? Buy 40 percent less food (especially the items you notice finding their way to the garbage)? Avoid sugared foods? Eat fewer meals of meat each week? Reuse plastic objects more than twice? More than three times? Keep your thermostat lower during the winter and higher during the summer? Buy locally? Buy *less*? Give up *more*?

Be sure to keep a journal on how it goes; record the numbers and the outcomes. After you take these first three steps, you'll find yourself knowledgeable, experienced, humbled, and proud of your values—all these are necessary, though not sufficient, qualities for convincing others.

If you've made it this far, please know that I am very proud of you for many reasons, not the least of which is that now you are ready for the hard part.

Step 4: *Can you make your personal investments consistent with your values?*

Investments can refer to stocks, bonds, mutual funds, but actually, every time you make a purchase you are investing in something. When you buy a cappuccino on the run, you are investing in the location of the café, how it treats its employees, the means by which it obtains coffee beans, the living conditions of the sourced milk cows, and the transport system that brought all those ingredients into your neighborhood. It's admittedly a bewildering challenge, but it's useful to think about which of the five things on that list conforms to your values and which ones do not. Can you patronize a café that meets two of your criteria, while you search for one that meets three? Baby steps. No one can run before they can walk.

Step 5: *Can you move your institutions toward consistency with your values?*

At this point you possess the magic criterion to advocate for change: personal experience. Go to your school, your house of worship, your place of employment, and start a dialogue with those in charge. Share your values, your struggles, and your experience. Listen to them talk about their restrictions and concerns. Thank them for their time. Write a follow-up letter emphasizing your values, your struggles, and your experience, and ask for another appointment. Talk to your peers within the institution. Keep going back, keep advocating for the things you believe in. It takes time and perseverance, but people (even politicians) and their institutions can change.

But you're only one person in a world of more than seven billion. Will changing your values make any difference?

11. THE DIFFERENCE YOU MAKE

Give me a big enough lever, and a place to stand
upon, and I will move the Earth.

—ARCHIMEDES (C. 250 BCE)

More than two thousand years ago, a man we remember as Archimedes claimed that he could move the entire Earth if he only had a big enough lever and a place to stand. He was talking about geometry, mass, and force, but his quotation works for global change as well. Making a difference as to energy is often about finding the biggest lever, figuring out where to stand, and then pushing and pulling like hell.

For better or worse, as a member of the Organisation for Economic Co-operation and Development (OECD), you are part of the biggest lever in the world when it comes to the issues raised in this book. The people of the OECD, while representing only one-sixth of the global population, use one-third of the world's energy and half of the world's electricity and are responsible for one-third of the world's carbon dioxide emissions. Not only that, but the OECD consumes one-third of the world's meat as well as one-third of the world's sugar.

For even better or even worse, America is by far the biggest lever within the OECD. With a population amounting to one-quarter of the OECD (and only 4 percent of the entire world), the United States uses half of the OECD's total energy and one-third of the OECD's total electricity and is responsible for just under half of the OECD's total carbon dioxide emissions. The United States also eats one-third of the OECD's total meat as well as one-quarter of the OECD's total sugar.

This means that if you are a citizen of the United States or any of the other OECD countries, any steps you take toward conservation will have an outsized effect on global consumption. Let me give you an example:

Let's say an examination of your values has led you to the belief that reducing carbon dioxide emissions is important. A fact-finding mission revealed that all of your household electricity comes from a coal-burning plant on the other side of town. Because at least 20 percent of the total energy we consume comes to us as electricity, you've decided to take action by cutting down on your home usage of electricity as much as possible. How to proceed?

A good way to start is to figure out the biggest lever in your home affecting electricity usage. In the European Union (EU), all new appliances are required to be sold bearing an EPREL sticker displaying several indices of energy efficiency. The critical value to look for is the number of "kWh/annum," which is the estimated amount of electricity the appliance will use during one year while serving a household of five. By comparing this number between makes and models, members of EU countries can begin to choose and control the level of energy use in their homes. Some American companies (General Electric, for example) provide kWh/year estimates for selected products, such as freezers and refrigerators. Additional companies could be lobbied to make this information more available.

For most homes and apartments around the world, it is by far the electric water heater that uses the most energy; having hot water usually amounts to about half of the total electricity used in your home. If you're able to change from a fifty-gallon water heater to a twenty-gallon model and use cooler water (or even cold water) while washing clothes, rinsing dishes, and taking showers, you can cut your water heater's electricity use by as much as half, meaning that you've now cut your total household electricity use by one-quarter.

The next biggest levers are the machines designed to heat large spaces and to cool them—that is, space heaters and air-conditioning units. Together, they probably eat up another one-third of your electric bill. If you can tolerate a decrease in room temperature during the cold season and an increase during the warm season, you will save energy. Note that your air conditioner is the bigger lever of the two: when cooling a room, you must vent the hot air of the room into the even hotter air outside, and moving against entropy requires extra energy. An air-conditioning unit will require about double the electricity of a space heater to achieve the same degree change in temperature in a given room. Can you go without A/C for more days of the year? How much can you turn the heat down during winter? In theory (with a fireplace and a fan), you could all but eliminate this heating/cooling lever. Now you've cut your total electricity use by 60 percent.

The next-biggest levers in your home are the objects that heat or cool small spaces: your clothes dryer, your stove, your dishwasher, and your refrigerator/freezer. All together they use about 15 percent of the total electricity in your home. Could you use them less often or run them at a different temperature? Admittedly, these are not strong levers, but every little bit counts.

Ironically, your television, your computer, and the lights that brighten your home—things you are probably careful to turn off when not using—contribute very little to your total electricity usage. You'd have to leave a sixty-watt light blazing 24/7 for a whole year to approach the amount of electricity your electric stove consumes off and on. For slobs like me, the bad news is that this set of weak levers also includes your vacuum cleaner. If you vacuum your house once a month instead of once a week, you've barely shaved off one-third of 1 percent from your total electricity use for the year.

Nonetheless, by making all these changes, you have now lowered your home electricity use by a whopping 70 percent. This lowers your tally from just over the average modern use in the OECD (ten megawatts per hour per year) to the 1965 average of Switzerland that I keep talking about. If each of the 1.3 billion people in the OECD made similar sacrifices, it would lower global electricity use by 25 percent and lower fossil fuel use and carbon dioxide emissions accordingly.

Maybe electricity use is not your thing; maybe you are more concerned with meat intake, or food waste, or car commuting, or airline travel, or pesticide use. Regardless of your mission, start in your own home and expand from there. I promise you'll be surprised at how far abroad it takes you.

The above may seem like an impossible task, but so did curing tuberculosis or putting a man on the moon or building the Great Wall across China or starting a new nation based on all men being equal or sailing across an unknown ocean in search of an unmapped land. History teaches us that these challenges were thoroughly overcome, via means honorable or shameful, despite the fact that they were originally deemed both ridiculous and impossible.

In most ways, we are just as noble and frail and flawed and ingenious as the people who cured and dared and built and forged centuries ago. Like them, we are ultimately endowed with only four resources: the earth, the ocean, the sky, and each other. If we can refrain from overestimating our likelihood of failure, then neither must we underestimate our capacity for success.

III. A SuMMARY OF FACTS

GLOBALLY, since 1969 . . .

. . . population has doubled.

. . . child mortality has decreased by half.

. . . average life expectancy has increased by twelve years.

. . . forty-seven cities have grown to contain more than ten million people.

. . . production of cereal grains has tripled.

. . . the amount of crops that can be harvested per acre has more than doubled.

. . . the amount of land cultivated for farming has increased by 10 percent.

. . . production of meat has tripled.

. . . annual slaughter of pigs has tripled; chicken has increased sixfold; cattle has increased by half.

. . . consumption of seafood has tripled.

. . . the amount of fish taken from the ocean has doubled.

. . . the invention of aquaculture made fish farming the source of half of all seafood eaten today.

. . . production of seaweed has increased tenfold; we eat half of the total as hydrocolloid food additives.

. . . consumption of table sugar has nearly tripled.

. . . the amount of human waste produced each day has more than doubled.

. . . waste of edible food has increased such that it now equals the amount of food needed to adequately feed all the undernourished people on Earth.

. . . the total amount of energy that people use every day has tripled.

. . . the total amount of electricity that people use every day has quadrupled.

. . . 20 percent of the world's population has come to use half of the world's electricity.

. . . the total population living with no access to electricity has grown to one billion people.

. . . the number of airline passengers has increased tenfold, while the total distance traveled by rail has declined.

. . . the miles traveled by car each year has more than doubled; there are currently almost one billion motor vehicles on the planet.

. . . global fossil fuel use has nearly tripled.

. . . coal and oil use has doubled; natural gas use has tripled.

. . . the invention of biofuels has grown to consume 20 percent of the global annual harvest of grain.

. . . the production of plastic has increased tenfold.

. . . the invention of new plastics has grown to consume 10 percent of the fossil fuels used each year.

. . . the share of electricity generated using hydropower has decreased to an all-time low of 15 percent.

. . . the share of electricity generated using nuclear power has increased to an all-time high of 6 percent.

. . . the adoption of wind- and solar-powered electricity has grown to provide almost 5 percent of all electricity generated each year.

. . . one trillion tons of carbon dioxide have been released into the atmosphere from the burning of fossil fuels.

. . . the average global surface temperature has increased by one degree Fahrenheit.

. . . the average global sea level has increased by four inches; half of this rise was due to the addition of water melted from mountain glaciers and polar ice.

. . . more than half of all amphibian, bird, and butterfly species has declined in population; one-quarter of all fish and plant species has declined in population.

IV. SOURCES AND SUGGESTED READING

Upon finishing this book, readers may be asking themselves, Where in the world did she find quantitative data on feed conversion in domestic poultry, the frequency of adolescent hockey games in Manitoba, the volume of nocturnal urine production in humans, and the employment history of railway workers in Spain (and so much more)? Amazingly, it's all out there if you just look for it! While researching this book, I discovered the delightful truth that a database for pretty much *everything* exists, and the more you search, the better you get at searching. So, before we're done, I want to share with you the sources that I used while researching and writing *The Story of More*, as well as some tips for pursuing your own research.

For many years, I have relied upon the Worldwatch Institute's publication *Vital Signs* (especially volumes 19, 20, 21, and 22) as a starting point for classroom discussions of the many issues presented in this book. These condensed guides to *The Trends That Are Shaping Our Future* are invaluable reading for anyone concerned about the future of our planet or curious about its past. Diverse organizations also consolidate climate change research for the public, such as Project Drawdown, a nonprofit coalition of scientists and entrepreneurs focused on the full suite of greenhouse gases, well beyond the basics of carbon dioxide that I presented here.

The numbers I have offered, as well as the ones I used to make calculations, were taken from several national and international public data sets and reports. I extensively used data archived by the many arms of the United Nations, including its Population Division (UNPD), Statistics Division, Departments of Economic and Social Affairs, Fisheries and Aquaculture, Human Settlements Program, Refugee Agency, and Global Happiness Council, as well as its Educational, Scientific and Cultural Organization (UNESCO), Food and Agriculture Organization, International Children's Emergency Fund (UNICEF), and World Health Organization (WHO). I also made use of the following UN reports: "Fish to 2030: Prospects for Fisheries and Aquaculture"; "2018 Revision of World Urbanization Prospects"; "Frequently Asked Questions on Climate Change and Disaster Displacement"; "Food Outlook" (2018); "OECD-FAO Agricultural Outlook 2018–2027"; and "A Guide to the Seaweed Industry."

I acquired additional data from several other international organizations, including the International Civil Aviation Organization, International Council for the Exploration of the Sea, International Energy Agency (IEA), Organisation for Economic Co-operation and

Development (OECD), National Hydropower Association, Organization for the Development of Fisheries, Observatory of Economic Complexity (OEC), Organization of Motor Vehicle Manufacturers (OICA), International Starch Institute, and International Union of Railways. The IEA publishes a useful report titled "World Energy Outlook"; the Natural Resources Defense Council published another detailed report, "Wasted: How America Is Losing Up to 40 Percent of Its Food from Farm to Fork to Landfill" (2012). The World Bank provided data sets, as did the Global Energy Observatory and Gapminder.org. Four private companies supplied international data sets: the British Petroleum Global compilation on energy use; the Malcolm Dunstan and Associates database of concrete dams throughout the world; PlasticsEurope (the Association of Plastics Manufacturers); and Elgiganten's database of energy efficiency for a multitude of home appliances.

The Intergovernmental Panel on Climate Change has published a series of assessment reports dated 1990, 1992 (supplement), 1995, 2001, 2007, and 2014, as well as a series of special reports on select topics including 2000 ("Emissions Scenarios"), 2012 ("Renewable Energy Sources and Climate Change Mitigation"), 2012 ("Managing the Risks of Extreme Events and Disasters to Advance Climate Change Adaptation"), 2018 ("Global Warming of 1.5°C"), and 2019 ("Climate Change and Land" and "The

Ocean and Cryosphere in a Changing Climate"). All of these were useful while researching this book.

Many of the examples in this book refer to the United States, the country of my birth. Data sets for these calculations were accessed from several branches of the United States Department of Agriculture (USDA), including the National Agricultural Statistics Service, Census of Agriculture, Economic Research Service, and Center for Nutrition Policy and Promotion, as well as Nationwide Food Surveys from 1935 to the present. Other US federal entities that provided data were the National Census, National Park Service, Federal Register of the National Archives, Central Intelligence Agency World Factbook, Energy Information Administration (EIA), National Aeronautics and Space Administration (NASA), Geological Survey, National Agricultural Library, National Center for Health Statistics (NCHS), American Petroleum Institute, and the Department of State's Office of the Historian.

The National Academies of Science, Engineering, and Medicine provided the following two relevant reports: "Resources and Man: A Study and Recommendations" (1969) and "Safety of Genetically Engineered Foods: Approaches to Assessing Unintended Health Effects" (2004). The Environmental Protection Agency (EPA) published a set of valuable reports that include "Pesticide Industry Sales and Usage: 2008–2012 Market Estimates" (2017); "Municipal Solid Waste Generation,

Recycling, and Disposal in the United States: Facts and Figures for 2012"; "Light-Duty Automotive Technology, Carbon Dioxide Emissions, and Fuel Economy Trends: 1975 Through 2017"; "U.S. Households' Demand for Convenience Foods"; "Sugar and Sweetener Report" (1976); and "Sugar and Sweeteners Yearbook." I also used the USDA report "Family Food Consumption and Dietary Levels for Five Regions" (1941) and the Department of Health and Human Services' "2015–2020 Dietary Guidelines for Americans," 8th ed.

State- and city-specific data came from documents provided by the city of Philadelphia, Iowa State University, Michigan State Highway Department, Minnesota Historical Society, and St. Paul Public Works.

The country of Norway, where I now make my home, was very helpful in supplying me with access to the following databases: Statistical Institute, Fisheries and Coastal Affairs, Oil and Energy Program—all departments within the Norwegian Ministry of Trade, Industry and Fisheries. Three reports were also useful: the Norwegian Seafood Federation's "Aquaculture in Norway"; "Norway's Petroleum History," courtesy of norskpetroleum.no; the Norwegian Centre for Climate Services report "Sea Level Change for Norway: Past and Present Observations and Projections to 2100"; and the Norwegian Environment Agency report "The Impacts of 1.5°C: A Science Briefing."

Many of the claims made in this book were verified

by news releases from PR Newswire, Reuters, and the USDA Newsroom. Several articles within periodicals were also used for this purpose. *The New York Times* was a preferred source of information, but the following sources also contributed: *The Atlantic*, Center for Science in the Public Interest, CNN, *Forbes*, Minneapolis *Star Tribune*, *National Geographic*, *National Review*, *Pacific Standard*, *Scientific American*, *Smithsonian*, *Vanity Fair*, and *The Washington Post*.

While researching *The Story of More*, I amassed a broad collection of the scientific literature, too many works to include here. However, I wish to note my reliance upon multiple works by the following scholars: Jonathan Bamber, Charles Benbrook, Mignon Duffy, Kerry Emanuel, John Harte, Ray Hilborn, Arjen Y. Hoekstra, Svetlana Jevrejeva, Matti Kummu, Tim Lenton, Diana Liverman, Katherine Meyer, Stuart Pimm, Barry Popkin, Roberto E. Reis, David B. Roy, William H. Schlesinger, Carl Schleussner, David Tilman, and David Vaughan. If I had to boil it down, under duress, to a recommendation of two works to be considered must-reads from the above, they would be the following:

1. New, Mark George, Diana Liverman, Heike Schroeder, and Kevin Anderson. "Four Degrees and Beyond: The Potential for a Global Temperature Increase of Four

Degrees and Its Implications." *Philosophical Transactions of the Royal Society A: Mathematical, Physical and Engineering Sciences* 369, no. 1934 (2011): 6–19.
2. Vaughan, Naomi E., and Timothy M. Lenton. "A Review of Climate Geoengineering Proposals." *Climatic Change* 109, nos. 3–4 (2011): 745–90.

For readers who may have caught the data bug, I want to recommend several aggregated resources where you can sift through international and national data on your own. I implore you not to put your research off, as there is no guarantee that these databases will exist next year, or next week, for that matter. Case in point: every two years since 2010, the EPA published a report titled "Climate Change Indicators in the United States." The 2010, 2012, 2014, and 2016 reports were invaluable public resources; they broke down the results of the state-of-the-art science clearly and accurately for lay readers, and illustrated trends using high-quality graphics. During the years 2018 and 2020, however, no report was produced and no explanation was given for the omission. As the leadership and priorities of our governments change, the type and amount of data that it chooses to make public may change also.

As of this writing, the World Bank maintains an open

data site (data.worldbank.org) where you can visualize and download population, health, economy, education, and development data collected by the UNPD, UNICEF, WHO, UNESCO, IDS, OECD, and others. The Food and Agriculture Organization (FAO) of the United Nations maintains the FAOSTAT open data site (fao.org/faostat) where you can download files of agricultural data describing the production and consumption of crops, livestock, and other foodstuffs for every country of the world.

You may be able to find out what kind of power plant serves your neighborhood via the EIA's comprehensive site listing power plant schedules (eia.gov/electricity/data/eia923). British Petroleum Global maintains a database (bp.com/en/global/corporate/energy-economics/statistical-review-of-world-energy.html) of the oil, coal, and gas use, production, and reserves, broken down by country, in addition to electricity use from both renewable and nonrenewable sources. For a comprehensive picture of each country's annual imports and exports, I recommend the Observatory of Economic Complexity's website (oec.world/en/profile/country/usa). The OECD's Data Department offers a site (data.oecd.org) where you can visualize and compare trends in passenger and freight transportation for each of the OECD countries and several others as well. The Organization of Motor Vehicle Manufacturers website (oica.net) offers downloadable data files describing production and sales statistics of cars and other vehicles all over the world.

The United States Department of Agriculture maintains a National Agricultural Statistics Service (quickstats.nass .usda.gov) where you can look up individual commodity yields for all plant and animal products produced in the United States, broken down by region, state, watershed, county, and zip code, as well as the Census of Agriculture website (nass.usda.gov/AgCensus/index.php), which offers data describing the size, status, and profit margin for the farms of America. The USDA also maintains a Foreign Agricultural Service (https://apps.fas.usda.gov/psdonline /app/index.html#/app/home) describing individual commodities in terms of imports versus exports for every country in the world. The National Center for Health Statistics (under the umbrella of the Centers for Disease Control and Prevention) offers myriad data (cdc.gov /nchs/pressroom/calendar/pub_archive.htm) describing the food intake habits of Americans between 2009 and 2018, as well as directions for accessing older data sets. Finally, the United States Census Bureau performs population and demographic surveys of America that catalog housing patterns, salary by profession, commuting times, and so much more (census.gov/programs-surveys /decennial-census/decade.2010.html).

I made several choices when I wrote this book, and those choices had ramifications for the story I've told.

I mostly dealt with global data sets, as I wanted to discuss trends that were truly global in scale. Unfortunately, some key data sets are incomplete: for my numerous discussions of global energy, zero data exists for approximately twenty countries out of the world's two hundred or so. What these twenty countries have in common is, first, they are located in sub-Saharan Africa and, second, they are very poor countries with per capita income less than 10 percent of the global average. As such, these countries can be safely assumed to use low amounts of energy relative to the rest of the world (for now), but we should also remember that they contain 260 million people in total—more than the population of Germany, France, Spain, and the United Kingdom combined.

There were many instances when I preferred to focus on the experience of women when relating the trends of the last fifty years. Usually, my reasons were obvious: maternal mortality is an exclusively female statistic. Sometimes they were more complex: my analysis of the gender gap and how it might relate to population growth reflects both my examination of the data and my own experiences as a woman and mother.

I singled out several individual countries for analysis, namely the United States for its outsized production and consumption of energy, corn, meat, sugar, and waste; Norway for the rapid evolution of its fishing industry; and Brazil for its ongoing loss of endemic species. The utility of dividing global data sets by country is rooted in the presumption that a sovereign nation is subject to a uniform economy and system of justice. For example, the country of Brazil is home to neither the greatest amount of forest (that would be Russia), nor the fastest-shrinking forest (that would be Indonesia). However, Brazil *is* home to the greatest amount of shrinking forest in the world, all of it under the purview of a single government. Thus judicial or economic changes in Brazil have an outsized effect on global trends in forested land area, making Brazil a critical talking point within any discussion of global deforestation.

The trouble with dividing global data sets by country also lies in the presumption that a sovereign nation is subject to a uniform economy and system of justice. While researching chapter 8 ("Making Sugar"), my foray into data sets that specified black versus white Americans revealed significant disparities. For example, according to a USDA report from 1936, the households of "negro families" in southeastern states contained only 70 percent as much staple sugar as the households of "white farm operators" living in the same region. Seventy years later, in 2006, the National Center for Health Statistics reported that black adults were consuming twice as much sugar as white adults in the form of sugared beverages. Similarly, my general history of women's work in the United States diverged from that of women of color: while it is true that the percentage of all mothers who were employed outside the home doubled, from 30 to 60 percent, between 1976 and 1998, it is also true that the percentage of unmarried women of color (a number of them mothers) employed outside the home has not been lower than 60 percent for more than one hundred years. Clearly, the general trends in American sugar consumption and female labor participation differ from the specific experience of Americans of color over the last several decades.

As the philosopher José Ortega y Gasset wrote in 1923, "To define is to exclude and negate." Any discussion of average trends effectively subsumes the experience of some, creating a picture that may be at odds with the experience of many. Analyses highlighting the history of individual countries and their subset populations will be the next step toward telling a fuller and more nuanced story than the one I presented here.

Finally, I wish to recognize the many farmers, foresters, ranchers, fishers, nutritionists, businesspeople, factory workers, scientists, and engineers who read sections of this book and helped me clear up my use of the terminology, history, and specific workings of their particular fields. From this group, I wish to especially note the generous assistance of Cory Arjes, Elena Bennett, Clint Conrad, Brenda Davy, Mat Domeier, Andy Elby, Pierre Kleiber, Moses Milazzo, Matthew Miller, Paul Richard, Adolf Schmidt, and Reidar Trønnes.

ACKNOWLEDGMENTS

My work on this book was encouraged and supported by many people, all of whom are very dear to me. Critical to this edition were two girls of Young Reader age who were kind enough to read the adult version of *The Story of More* and give me comments as to which parts were more (and less) interesting from their perspective. It was their feedback that formed the compass I followed as I revised the original. Their names are Norah Ohly and Waverly Van Buren. I turned to Tina Bennett for guidance countless times while writing this book and benefited enormously from her insight and experience. LuAnn Walther, my editor at Vintage, just plain *gets me* (it's an Iowa thing), and I am so grateful to her. Robin Desser and Ursula Doyle are women whom I have come to rely upon for thoughtful answers and careful eyes. Every author should have a trusted friend who reads her first drafts and gently steers her toward what she does best; for me, that person is Svetlana Katz. Thirty-five years ago, Connie Luhmann and I sat side by side and learned grammar and shorthand from the same chalkboard. Who would have guessed that those two girls would grow up to be us, still diagramming sentences together, still as close as sisters? Adrian Nicole LaBlanc continues to be generous in sharing her wisdom and experience with both writing and authorship.

There were two people who particularly encouraged me in this project but did not live to see it come to completion. Professor Fred Duennebier and the Reverend Fritz Fritschel steadily assured me of the importance and necessity of this book and of their faith in me as its author. My grief in losing them is tempered by my pride in following through. I am also indebted to each and every person—especially the good people at the Lutheran Church of Honolulu—who asked me when the next book was coming out. Your enthusiasm gave me permission to feed my fondest indulgence and call it "work," and I can never thank you enough. Last but not least, I want to thank whoever graffitied the electrical box at the corner of Blindernveien and Apalveien with: "We worship an invisible god and slaughter a visible nature—without realizing that this nature we slaughter is the invisible god we worship." It got me to thinking.

ABOUT THE AUTHOR

HOPE JAHREN is an award-winning scientist who has been pursuing independent research in paleobiology since 1996. She is the author of two works of nonfiction: *The Story of More* and the bestselling *Lab Girl*. Recognized by *Time* magazine in 2016 as one of the 100 most influential people in the world, Jahren is the recipient of three Fulbright Awards and served as a tenured professor at the University of Hawaii in Honolulu from 2008 to 2016, where she built the isotope geobiology laboratories. She currently holds the J. Tuzo Wilson Professorship at the University of Oslo, Norway.

thestoryofmore.com
hopejahrensurecanwrite.com
jahrenlab.com
@HopeJahren